H. W. Parker

Snakes
a natural history

Second edition

Revised and enlarged by A. G. C. Grandison

Illustrator: B. C. Groombridge

British Museum (Natural History)

Cornell University Press

ITHACA AND LONDON

First edition published 1965, under the title
Natural History of Snakes

Second edition, revised by A. G. C. Grandison, first published 1977 by the British Museum (Natural History) and Cornell University Press.

International Standard Book Number (cloth) 0-8014-1095-9
International Standard Book Number (paper) 0-8014-9164-9
Library of Congress Catalog Card Number 76-54625

Colour printed by W. S. Cowell Ltd,
The Butter Market Ipswich
Text printed in Great Britain by Butler & Tanner Ltd,
Frome and London

Contents

Acknowledgements

While correcting and updating the text of the first edition I have received assistance from many persons, notably E. Nicholas Arnold and Garth L. Underwood both of whom critically read the first draft and provided information and ideas, and Andrew F. Stimson who compiled the index and glossary and helped in many other ways.

I am also conscious of my indebtedness to my friends and colleagues Charles M. Bogert, Donald G. Broadley, Nathan W. Cohen, Gerald T. Dunger, Carl Gans, Geoffrey Kinns, John D. Romer and John H. Tashjian who responded most willingly and generously to my appeal for photographs.

Most of the line drawings were prepared by Brian C. Groombridge, a postgraduate student in zoology.

I wish also to acknowledge the kindness of colleagues and publishing houses in the United States for allowing re-drawing of some figures that appear in their publications.

To all those who helped produce this second edition I express my gratitude.

A. G. C. Grandison

1 *The origin and orders of living reptiles*

The origin of reptiles

Although the fossil remains of living creatures of the past can never reveal more than a fraction of the whole history of life on earth, they nevertheless indicate, almost beyond doubt, that there were no backboned animals living on land before the Devonian period which began about 415 million years ago. There were, it is true, fishes that probably had lungs, like the present-day lungfishes (dipnoans), but there were no animals that had both lungs and true legs. Late in Devonian times, however, some small animals appeared that probably looked rather like salamanders. Known as the Ichthyostegalia, they had some fish-like characters, but they also had short limbs with five fingers and toes, i.e. pentadactyl. Although they seem to have been essentially aquatic creatures living in fresh water, they were probably capable of brief forays out of water or even of migrating overland for short distances when the pools they were living in dried up.

The remains of many similar animals have been found in the rocks of the earlier part of the next geological period (the Carboniferous 370–280 million years ago) and towards the end of it some related forms appeared that may well have been capable of longer sojourns on land. They almost certainly, however, had an aquatic larval stage like most of the modern Amphibia ; but in the same geological period some apparently fully terrestrial vertebrates appeared. These animals differed considerably from the amphibians of the period and had resemblances to the modern reptiles, but their precise antecedents are a matter of conjecture. There are no indications of any pre-existing stock that had both lungs and pentadactyl limbs except the Amphibia, and it is therefore assumed that some of the very early members of this group acquired modifications that enabled them to dispense with an aquatic stage entirely.

Animals with a combination of reptilian and amphibian features occurred early in the Permian, the best known being *Seymouria* which older textbooks treated as the classic example of a stem reptile. However *Seymouria* existed not only too recently to have been ancestral to the reptiles, but its skeleton, and particularly

GEOLOGICAL TIME-SCALE†

AGE IN MILLIONS OF YEARS	GEOLOGICAL SYSTEMS (Maximum thickness in metres)			TIME RANGES OF LIFE GROUPS

QUATERNARY*

AGE IN MILLIONS OF YEARS	SYSTEM	Max thickness	ERA	LIFE GROUPS
1·8*→	PLIOCENE	5000 m	CAENOZOIC ‡	
5·5 →	MIOCENE	7000 m		
22·5 →	OLIGOCENE	9000 m		
36·0 →	EOCENE	10 000 m		
53·5 →	PALAEOCENE	4000 m		
65·0 →				
	CRETACEOUS	17 000 m	MESOZOIC	
135 →				
	JURASSIC	15 000 m		
200 →				
	TRIASSIC	10 000 m		
240 →				
	PERMIAN	6000 m	PALAEOZOIC	
280 →				
	CARBONIFEROUS	19 000 m		
370 →				
	DEVONIAN	13 000 m		
415 →				
	SILURIAN	11 000 m		
445 →				
	ORDOVICIAN	13 000 m		
515 →				
	CAMBRIAN	13 000 m		
590 →				
	Unknown thickness		PROTEROZOIC	
	PRE-CAMBRIAN			
	Unknown thickness		AZOIC	
Origin of Earth's Crust 4500 →				

Life groups (columns, left to right): LAND PLANTS, PROTISTA, INVERTEBRATE ANIMALS, AGNATHANS AND FISHES, AMPHIBIANS, REPTILES, BIRDS, MAMMALS, MAN

† Time-Scale approximate with probable error ±5% throughout
* Quaternary (Pleistocene and Holocene) 2000 m
‡ Caenozoic –Tertiary (Palaeocene - Pliocene) + Quaternary
Column proportional to time-scale

the position and arrangement of the bones and openings associated with the middle ear, support the belief that it was an amphibian. The small, unspecialized lizard-like captorhinomorphs are more likely to be the ancestors of all reptile groups and its oldest member, *Hylonomus* from the Middle Carboniferous deposits of Nova Scotia, is undoubtedly a reptile.

From these early stages arose the great wealth of reptile life that dominated the earth's surface up to the end of the Cretaceous epoch, some 65 million years ago; and in the same line of descent are the relatively few groups of reptiles that have survived to the present day – the crocodiles and alligators, tortoises and turtles, lizards, amphisbaenians (formerly regarded as a group of burrowing lizards) and snakes, and the unique Tuatara.

It is, of course, possible to compare little more than the skeletons of the early and extinct forms of air-breathing vertebrates, but other structural differences can be compared in their living descendants. Some of these are compared in Table 1 and from this it can be seen that the reptiles have a greater number of features in common with the birds, which arose from them probably in Jurassic times (200–135 million years ago), than with their other and earlier descendants – the mammals, which first appear in the fossil record of Triassic times (240–200 million years ago) – or with their immediate forebears, the amphibians.

How reptiles differ from amphibians

Many of the features in which the reptiles differ from the amphibians are clearly associated with the suppression of an aquatic larval stage – the earliest reptiles being primarily terrestrial creatures. Further, because of the buoyancy of an aquatic environment, a massive and heavy skeleton is less of a handicap than for a terrestrial animal and one of the more obvious features of the evolutionary history of the reptiles is the progressive reduction of the ponderous skull and skeleton that they inherited from their amphibian ancestors.

The skull of the early amphibians and reptiles is virtually a half cone of heavy bones rigidly united with each other. It accommodates a tiny brain, the organs of smell, sight, hearing and balance, and the air passages from the nostrils to the mouth; its upper surface has openings for the eyes, nostrils, ears and, sometimes, the pineal organ, whilst the lower surface – the palate – has openings for the air passages from the nostrils, its edges forming the upper jaw.

Amongst modern reptiles the marine turtles have a skull that is still essentially of this pattern (fig. 1), though it contains fewer bones than more primitive types. But in almost all the other forms the massive bony canopy is reduced in extent. In tortoises this has been achieved by emargination of the hind part of the side of the skull and of the canopy above the ear, leaving a single 'arcade'

3

Some characters of recent air-breathing vertebrates

TABLE 1

	amphibians	reptiles	birds	mammals
1 Number of condyles for articulation of the skull and backbone	2	1*	1	2
2 Number of bones composing the lower jaw	2–5	3–7	5	1
3 Sound conducting bones of middle ear	1	1	1	3
4 Lower jaw articulates on	quadrate	quadrate	quadrate	squamosal
5 Number of heart ventricles	1	1 (2)	2	2
6 Aortic arches	2	2	1 (right)	1 (left)
7 Blood temperature	variable	variable	constant	constant
8 Larval stage	+(−)	−	−	−
9 Gills	+(−)	−	−	−
10 Fertilization	Ext. (int.)	internal	internal	internal
11 Male copulatory organs	−(+)	+(−)	−(+)	+
12 Membranes (amnion and allantois) around embryo	−	+	+	+
13 Skin covering	naked	scales	feathers	hairs
14 External openings for waste products	1	1	1	2

Symbols + and − indicate presence or absence and where both appear the condition shown first is the more usual.

*three in *Bolyeria*

between the upper jaw and the part of the skull on which the lower jaw hinges; in some forms this arcade is reduced to vanishing point. In the crocodiles and alligators, however, and in the Tuatara, two holes (fossae), one above the other, have been developed in the temporal canopy, leaving two arcades. In crocodiles the holes are small and the arcades massive, but in the Tuatara the original sheet of bone behind the orbit is reduced to a mere framework.

The process has gone even further in lizards and snakes. In the more typical lizards the upper of the two arcades persists, but in many of the burrowing lizards and in all the snakes both arcades are lost, thus leaving the quadrate bone, on which the lower jaw hinges, unsupported except for a connection at its lower end with one of the bones of the palate (the pterygoid) (fig. 1). Development and elaboration of skull openings in the temporal region have provided more spacious accommodation for the jaw muscles.

The reptilian orders

Although it might appear from fig. 1 that there are very considerable differences between a typical lizard and a typical snake these are selected instances and, as will become clear in the next chapter, there are, in fact, few clear-cut lines of distinction between the two groups. But they possess a number of features in common that are not found in any other extant reptiles except the burrowing amphisbaenians and so these three groups are usually brigaded together in the single 'order' SQUAMATA, comparable with the orders CROCODYLIA (crocodiles, alligators, False gharial, Gharial and caimans), TESTUDINES (tortoises, terrapins and turtles) and RHYNCHOCEPHALIA (Tuatara).

Some of the differences and resemblances between these orders may be mentioned briefly to illustrate the diverse methods which the present-day reptiles have developed in connection with the essentials of living. Thus, the Squamata are unique amongst reptiles in two features connected with their reproduction; the male copulatory organs are paired and the young have a tooth (or rarely a pair of teeth) which is used solely for the purpose of rupturing the egg membrane and is then shed. In the Tuatara the copulatory organ is absent but in all the other orders it is single, and the function of the egg-tooth is performed by a horny caruncle that grows on the tip of the snout. And there are notable differences in the other teeth of the different orders. The Testudines, of course, have no teeth, their place being taken by very effective cutting and grinding surfaces on the beak-like horny plates that cover the jawbones and which grow continuously to compensate for wear.

5

6

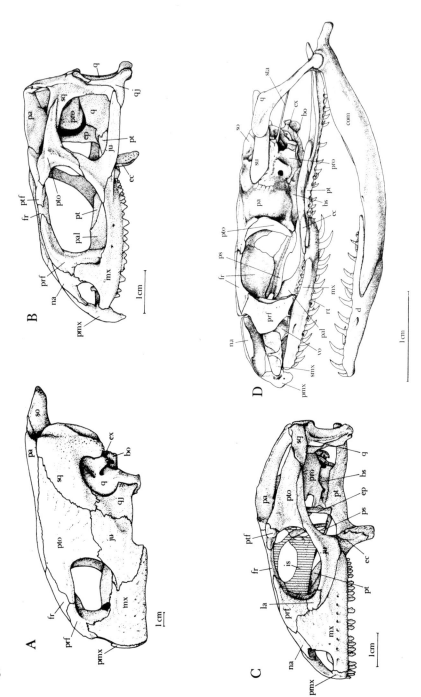

Tooth implantation and replacement

All other reptiles have one or other of three basic types of tooth implantation (fig. 2). The teeth of crocodilians have long cylindrical bases set in deep sockets on the crests of the jaws (thecodont type). Replacement teeth develop in shallow pockets alongside the bases of the functional teeth and by penetrating openings on the inner (lingual) side of these bases work their way up into the pulp cavities. In adult Tuataras cutting surfaces are developed in a different way. The teeth migrate from the inner sides of the jawbones to the crests where they fuse with the jawbone (acrodont type) and with each other, thus forming a series of chisel-shaped teeth. In time they may become completely worn down but there is apparently no replacement.

A somewhat similar acrodont type of implantation occurs in the agamid lizards (except in the front teeth), in chameleons and in one group of amphisbaenians, and once the teeth have reached a certain stage of development replacement is rare. In all other lizards as well as in snakes and in the other group of amphisbaenians the lingual wall of the jaw crest is reduced, leaving a high outer wall surface to which the teeth are fused (pleurodont type).

Replacement of the functional teeth follows a basic pattern of series of waves progressing along alternately numbered tooth series, one wave replacing the odd-numbered teeth followed by a second wave that brings about replacement of the even-numbered teeth and so on. These replacement rhythms usually continue throughout the reptile's life and as many as three or four replacement teeth may accompany every functional tooth. The sequence is from back to front in lizards and in all the non-venomous snakes, as well as the sea snakes, but it may be reversed in most other elapids and in the viperids.

Fig. 1. Lateral views of the skulls of: A. Turtle (*Chelonia mydas*). B. Tuatara (*Sphenodon punctatus*). C. Lizard (*Cyclura carinata*). D. Snake (*Ptyas mucosus*). The primitive type of reptile skull, exemplified by the turtle, has no temporal opening (anapsid condition) while the Tuatara has two openings bounded by bony arcades (diapsid condition). In lizards the lower of these arcades is lost by reduction of the lower arm of the jugal and loss of the quadratojugal (modified diapsid), and in snakes both arcades are lost. The cartilaginous interorbital septum is shown (vertical hatching) only in the lizard.

Key to abbreviations used in skull drawings

ang	angular	**fr**	frontal	**pmxt**	premaxillary teeth	**rt**	replacement tooth
bo	basioccipital	**is**	interorbital septum	**prf**	prefrontal	**smx**	septomaxilla
bs	basisphenoid			**pro**	prootic	**so**	supraoccipital
bt	basipterygoid process	**ju**	jugal	**ps**	parasphenoid	**sp**	splenial
		la	lachrymal	**pt**	pterygoid	**sq**	squamosal
co	coronoid	**lig**	ligament	**ptf**	postfrontal	**sta**	stapes
com	compound	**mx**	maxilla	**pto**	postorbital	**su**	supratemporal
d	dentary	**na**	nasal	**q**	quadrate	**vo**	vomer
ec	ectopterygoid	**pa**	parietal	**qj**	quadratojugal		
ep	epipterygoid	**pal**	palatine	**rfa**	replacement fang		
ex	exoccipital	**pmx**	premaxilla				
fa	fang						

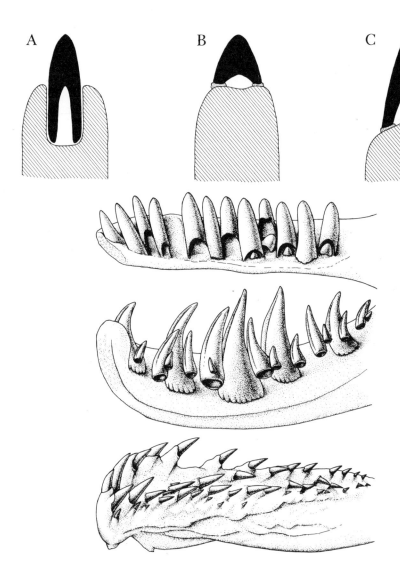

Fig. 2. Above. Diagram of the three basic types of tooth implantation in modern reptiles: A. Thecodont; B. Acrodont; C. Pleurodont. Key: Tooth (black); bone of attachment (stipple); jaw bone
(diagonal hatching).
Below. The positions of functional and replacement teeth in the Squamata. Top: Night lizard
(Xantusia vigilis). Centre: Gila monster. *(Heloderma suspectum)*. Bottom: Anaconda *(Eunectes murinus)*;
the soft gum tissue has not been fully removed from the jaw. (Based on Edmund 1960, and Edmund
1969 *in* Gans *et al.*)

Some of the characters in which lizards and snakes
(the Squamata) differ from other living reptiles

TABLE 2

	Crocodylia	Testudines	Rhyncho-cephalia	Squamata
1 Temporal fossae	+	−	+	+
2 Temporal arcades	2	1(o)	2	1(o)
3 Quadrato-jugal bone	+	+	+	−
4 Pineal eye	−	−	+	+(−)
5 Transverse hinge lines across the skull	−	−	−	+(−)
6 Teeth thecodont (t), pleurodont (p) or acrodont (a)	t	−	a	p(a)
7 Egg-tooth (t) or caruncle (c)	c	c	c	t
8 Urinary bladder	−	+	+	+(−)
9 Bony armour in skin	+	+	−	+(−)
10 Male copulatory organs	1	1	o	2
11 Arterial arch from which the subclavian artery arises	carotid	carotid	systemic	systemic

Symbols + and − indicate presence or absence and where both appear the condition shown first is the more usual.

The position and development of the replacement teeth vary; for instance the bases of the functional teeth of geckos, night lizards and iguanid lizards have cavities on their lingual surfaces which receive the replacement teeth as they develop while in other lizards the replacements lie lingual but slightly posterior to the precursors and no pits are produced in the old teeth for their reception. In snakes the replacement teeth lie flat on the lingual side of the bases of the functional teeth and facing backwards. When the old tooth is ready to be shed the tip of the new tooth swings upwards and the entire tooth migrates sideways and upwards into its predecessor's position (fig. 2).

Origin of the Squamata

Table 2 shows these and some of the other distinguishing features of the orders of living reptiles and it can be seen that the Squamata have more in common with the Rhynchocephalia than with either of the other two. The Rhynchocephalia, formerly a much more diverse and abundant group than they are today, were in existence in early Triassic times (240–220 million years ago), but they could not have been the ancestors of the Squamata, which already appear in the fossil record in late Permian and early Triassic times. The most that can be said with certainty is that the two groups are in the same line of descent from the extinct lizard-like eosuchians which existed in Permian times.

2 Lizards and snakes

The earliest snake

The origin of snakes is largely speculative and little documented. Their fossil record is scanty and in the great majority of cases based only on vertebrae; nevertheless it is now accepted that snakes arose from lizards, although no specific designation of the ancestral group can yet be made. The earliest remains clearly recognizable as belonging to a snake are those of *Lapparentophis defrennei* from the Lower Cretaceous (about 130 million years ago) of the Sahara. Although only its vertebrae have been found their distinctive features are unquestionably snake-like.

The most significant and complete fossil snake is another terrestrial form, *Dinilysia patagonica* (fig. 3), which was recovered from Upper Cretaceous sandstone beds in Argentina. It measures 1·8 metres and bears a number of similarities to some primitive extant snakes such as *Anilius* and *Cylindrophis* (see p. 63), but it also has several lizard-like characters, which however do not occur in any modern lizards, as well as unique features, such as the oval jaw joint, that are not seen in snakes, amphisbaenians or lizards.

The characteristics of snakes

The most obvious characters of snakes in general are the absence, or apparent absence, of limbs and their elongated flexible body with no sharp differentiation of neck, thorax, abdomen and so forth. No snake has any trace of forelimbs or a shoulder girdle (i.e. shoulder blades, collar bones, etc.) or of a breast bone, and in the vast majority there are no vestiges of hind limbs or a pelvis either; only in the boas and pythons and three other small groups are there persistent remains of hind limbs, which usually appear externally as small horn-sheathed claws (fig. 4), and some vestiges of a pelvis inside the ribs. Reduction of limbs to the same extent also occurs, however, in amphisbaenians and in some lizards (e.g. Slow-worm, Glass-lizard, etc.) and these, like the snakes, progress mainly by sinuous side-to-side undulations of the body in much the same way that an eel swims.

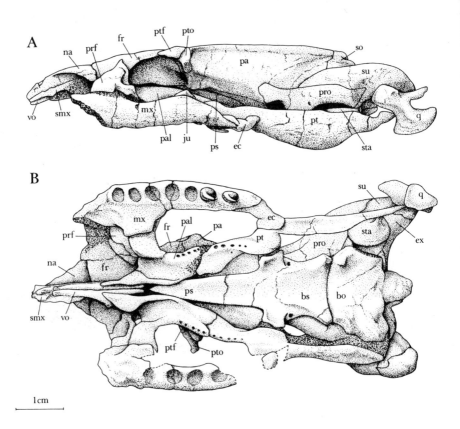

Fig. 3. Skull of one of the earliest fossil snakes, *Dinilysia patagonica* from the Upper Cretaceous. A. Lateral view. B. Ventral view. The premaxilla is missing. (Based on Estes, Frazzetta and Williams 1970). Key to abbreviations p. 7.

Locomotion

Serpentine locomotion. This type of 'serpentine' locomotion results from the passage of a series of waves that originate at the head and travel backwards. If there is nothing to impede the passage of the waves as, for instance, when a snake is placed on a sheet of polished glass, no progress results; but if there are obstacles, stones, twigs, vegetation or merely irregularities of the ground, the waves in their passage press against them and this pressure pushes the animal forwards.

12

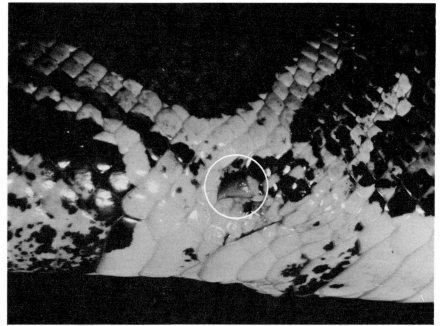

Fig. 4. Right side of the base of the tail of a Boa Constrictor (*Boa constrictor*) showing the horny spur at the side of the vent, also the enlarged ventral plates (gastrosteges). Most primitive snakes have such vestiges of hind limbs.

Photo: British Museum (Natural History): courtesy Zoological Society of London

Fig. 5, drawn from photographs taken at one-second intervals, shows the progress of a snake moving slowly across a board studded with regularly spaced pegs. The undulations of the body are not all exactly similar but it will be seen that the pegs with which the snake is in contact (solid black) all bear the same relationship to the bodywaves; each wave is in contact with pegs on its outer and hind side only. It will also be seen that the position of the waves relative to the background remains nearly constant and that the snake is 'flowing' past them; the asterisk on the middle of its back has moved from a position near the apex of a left-hand wave to a position nearly 7·5 cm farther forward at the apex of a right-hand wave.

The flexing of the body to create the waves is produced by muscles lying on either side of the backbone and attached to the sides of the individual vertebrae; short muscles connect adjacent vertebrae and longer ones span several, up to thirty or sometimes even more. A single wave of the Grass snake in fig. 5 is shown diagrammatically in fig. 6 and from this it can be seen that as the spot marked with an asterisk advances from grid-line D to E the muscles of the left-hand side near it change over from a condition of extension (M.E.) to one of contraction (M.C.). In between, in the region marked A.C., the muscles are

13

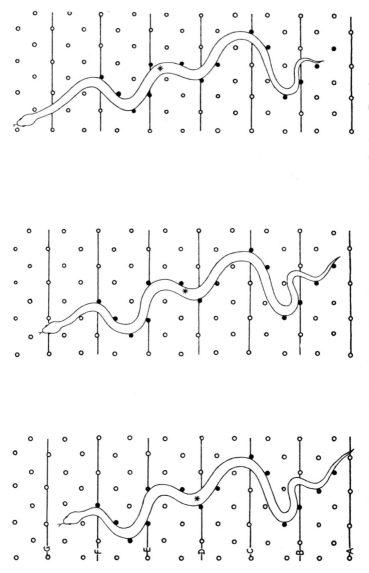

Fig. 5. A Grass snake (*Natrix natrix*) moving slowly across a board dotted with fixed pegs. Drawing by Parker 1965 after Gray and based on photographs taken at intervals of one second. Grid lines were 76mm apart.

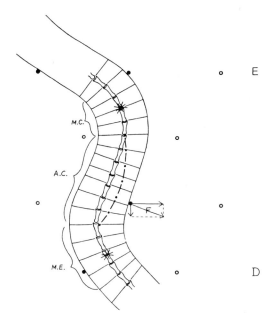

Fig. 6. Action of the muscles and the forces generated in a single wave of the snake in fig. 5. M.E. muscles extended; M.C. muscles contracted; A.C. muscles actively contracting; F. force acting against a resistance point, resolved. Drawing by Parker 1965.

actively contracting and it is when this is happening, and only then, that a muscle exerts a force. Since the backbone is not compressible the muscles attached to it could only shorten their length by bending it to a position in-dicated by the dotted line. Any such bending is, however, resisted by the fixed peg on the right-hand side so that the force exerted by the contracting muscles generates a pressure directed obliquely backwards and sideways against the peg (F). The lateral component of this pressure, normal to the surface, is absorbed by the peg, but the backward component, at right angles to it, pushes the snake forwards.

So, contraction of the muscles on the inner side of each loop of the body tends to alter the curvature, but if this is resisted by fixed objects on the substratum the force of the muscular contractions pushes the animal forwards along its own sinuous track, which is to some extent selected visually but is mainly determined by contact. Waves originate from the anterior end of the body and travel back-wards along its length without producing any propulsive effect until they encounter a resistance point; when resistance is met the wave is halted and the snake slides forwards.

Thus, greater length will be an advantage because it will allow more waves to exert their force at an increased number of 'footholds' simultaneously, and long, slender species are usually more efficient and swifter than shorter, stouter forms. But the speeds that snakes can achieve are often exaggerated. The darting movements of their heads when they are excited are exceptionally quick and so are their powers of acceleration from a standstill; but their maximum speed is low on account of the frictional resistance of the long sliding body. Although a Grass snake can exert a tractive effort equal to about a third of its own weight when moving freely under ideal conditions, it cannot attain more than about 6·5 km/h, whilst the Coachwhip snake, one of the swiftest species of North America, has been timed at 5·8 km/h and is probably capable of no more than 8–10 km/h and that only for a very short burst.

The requirements for 'serpentine' locomotion – a long, slender, highly flexible body in which the trunk muscles alone supply all the forces required for locomotion – involve a number of other modifications. Increase in length without loss of flexibility requires an increase in the number of vertebrae and in snakes the number varies from about 180 in the shorter, stouter forms to around 400 in some of the more attenuated species; even in snake-like lizards there may be more than 200. And the vertebrae themselves need reinforcing to withstand the strains and stresses engendered by the powerful trunk muscles. The usual articulation between vertebrae is a ball and socket joint with two pairs of interlocking projections that prevent the vertebrae from rotating on one another and so wringing the spinal cord and all the veins, arteries and nerves that run alongside the backbone.

In reptiles each backwardly directed projection has a downward facing flat surface (postzygapophysis, fig. 7) that slides over a similar, but upward facing, facet on the anterior prominence of the next vertebra (prezygapophysis). But snakes and four families of lizards have in addition a pair of outward facing facets (zygosphenes) between the prezygapophyses that fit into recesses with inward facing facets (zygantra) at the back of the adjacent vertebra. This tenon and mortise arrangement provides additional strength to resist torsion and restricts vertical bending to not more than about 30 degrees, but allows lateral flexure, on which locomotion depends, to nearly double this extent.

Rectilinear creeping. Propulsion by lateral undulations of the body is the basic form of locomotion in all the limbless Squamata but many terrestrial snakes have another, and unique, method of creeping which depends upon the action of muscles attached to the ribs and the skin of the belly and lower flanks.

From about the middle of each rib a muscle originates and runs obliquely backwards and downwards to be inserted on the skin, whilst another muscle originates at the lower end of the rib and runs forwards and is also inserted on the

16

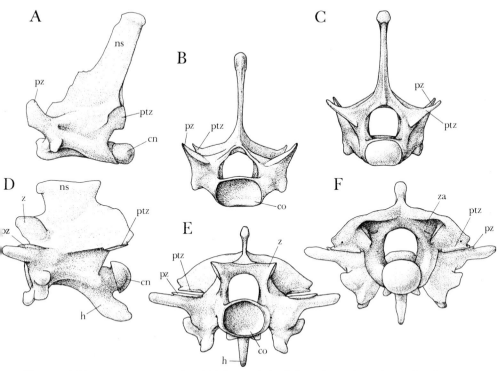

Fig. 7. A–C. Vertebra of an agamid lizard *(Calotes versicolor)* in lateral, anterior and posterior views. D–F. Vertebra of a colubrid snake *(Natrix natrix)* in lateral, anterior and posterior views. **cn** condyle; **co** cotyle; **h** hypapophysis; **ns** neural spine; **ptz** postzygapophysis; **pz** prezygapophysis; **za** zygantrum; **z** zygosphene.

skin. Contraction of the first muscle, the rib remaining stationary, will hitch the skin forwards at its point of insertion, with a slight lifting action since the muscle originates above its insertion, and contraction of a forwardly directed muscle from a rib farther back will restore it to its original position. But since the second muscle lies almost parallel with the belly there will be no lifting action.

So, when one of the backwardly directed muscles contracts, the scales of the belly and flanks where it is inserted are drawn forwards, sliding over the ground and becoming bunched up with the scales in front of them. When the second muscle comes into operation, however, the backwardly directed free edges of the scales are not lifted and tend to dig into the ground or to catch on any irregularities. The force of the muscle's contraction acting against this resistance will then draw the snake's body forwards.

In this 'rectilinear creeping' the backwardly directed muscles of each pair of ribs contract in a regular sequence, beginning just behind the head, and this wave of contractions is closely followed by a similar sequence of contractions of the opposite muscles. Several of these dual waves may follow one another at short intervals along the snake's body and combine to produce a slow, slug-like crawl.

The efficacy of this method of progression obviously depends to a large extent upon the scales which transmit the thrust and which act in much the same way as the pawls of a ratchet; if the pawls do not engage the mechanism fails. To ensure that the scales have the best chance of securing a purchase it is vital that they project, and at a sufficient but not too great an angle. Their normal overlapping arrangement inclines them at a slight angle, with their free, hinder, margins projecting a little; but the degree of inclination and projection is variable and controlled by a series of short muscles that connect scale with scale. These muscles, present in all snakes, represent the 'rectus superficialis' complex that occurs in some groups of lizards (where it also assists in locomotion) but has been lost in others.

The mechanism will also fail if the 'pawls' are not robust enough and the tips of pointed lanceolate scales, such as those normally present on a snake's back, would almost certainly buckle if subjected to a thrust sufficient to push the body forward. Most terrestrial snakes therefore have enlarged scales (gastrosteges) arranged in a single longitudinal row along the belly (fig. 4). Each of them corresponds with a single vertebra (and a pair of ribs) and normally each is as broad as the belly. This transverse enlargement allows the muscles from the ribs of both sides to be inserted at the outer ends of each scute and act as a pair to produce a median thrust; without this arrangement the muscles, being off-centre, would have turning moments whenever the scales of one side, but not those of the other, secured a foothold.

Sidewinding, a method of locomotion employed by several snakes living in sandy deserts, is described on p. 34.

Internal modifications

Attenuation also involves modification and rearrangement of the contents of the abdominal cavity. The alimentary canal becomes an almost straight tube, coiled only in the region of the small intestine, with the stomach a simple enlargement; the liver is narrow, with the right lobe considerably longer than the left, and the gall bladder is displaced backwards to lie behind it; the kidneys are also elongated and their arrangement is staggered, the right lying farther forward than the left; and the testes and ovaries are also staggered in the same way or the left oviduct may be absent.

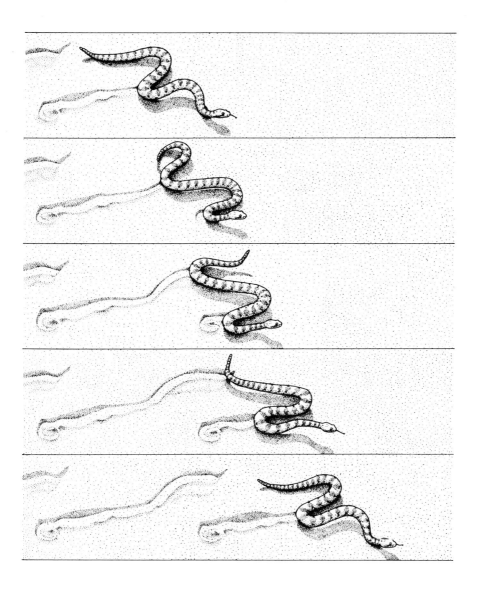

Fig. 8. Stages in sidewinding locomotion based on a film strip. Top frame is the earliest in the sequence and progression is from left to right. (Modified from Gans 1974.)

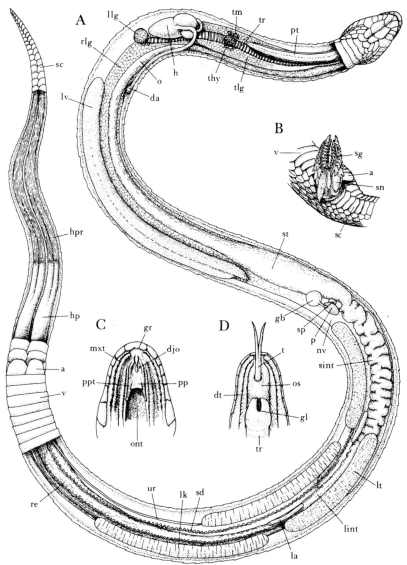

Fig. 9. Snake anatomy. A. Ventral view of *Waglerophis merremii*. Most of ventral and subcaudal scales removed. B. Right everted hemipenis of Adder *(Viper berus)*. C. Palate of Dhaman *(Ptyas mucosus)*. D. Floor of mouth of *Ptyas mucosus* showing partially extruded tongue and protrusible glottis. *Key to abbreviations on facing page.*

The organs most affected, however, are the lungs and the urinary bladder. In several groups of lizards when limbs are reduced in size and locomotion is 'serpentine', the left lung is appreciably smaller than the other but in none of them has it disappeared entirely.* A few snakes also have two lungs but in the vast majority the left is either vestigial or absent. The capacity of the right lung is increased by a backward extension that is thin-walled and lacks the normal alveolar lung structure, but additional respiratory area is provided by a new structure derived from the windpipe – the vascular lining of the lung extends forwards on to the roof of the trachea. Development of such a tracheal lung is usually accompanied by a reduction in the vascular area of the true lung. In some aquatic snakes the lung extends nearly as far back as the vent and additionally acts as a hydrostatic organ. The urinary bladder has disappeared and only at the embryonic stage is there a solution of urea. The adult snake voids its nitrogenous waste in a semi-solid state that is mainly composed of uric acid.

Sensory and skeletal comparisons

Other features in which typical snakes differ appreciably from typical lizards, but in most of which there is no clear-cut line of distinction between the two groups, are to be found in some of the sense organs and in the structure of the skull.

Eyes. Snakes' eyes have no movable eyelids, but the cornea is protected by a transparent area of the general integument. Usually this area is a separate and distinct circular transparent spectacle (the brille) covering the eye alone, but sometimes it is a circular patch in a larger scale. Lizards' eyes typically have three movable eyelids (upper, lower and nictitating membrane), but some forms with burrowing or semi-burrowing habits have a brille and others show stages in the development of this peculiarity. Various stages can be found in which the centre of the still movable lower lid becomes progressively more transparent so that the animal can see even with its eyes 'shut'; in the next stage the lower lid, with a window, remains permanently in the closed position and finally the upper margin of the lower lid becomes fused to the lower edge of the upper lid. There are also notable differences in the structure of the eyes themselves. In typical diurnal lizards focussing is brought about, as in the human eye, by

* In the amphisbaenians, there is usually only one lung, and it is the right that has been lost.

---

a anal scale (divided in *Waglerophis*); **da** dorsal aorta (only anterior portion); **djo** duct of Jacobson's organ of left side; **dt** dentary teeth; **gb** gall bladder; **gl** glottis; **gr** groove in rostral scale to facilitate tongue protrusion; **h** heart; **hp** hemipenis; **hpr** hemipenis retractor muscle (arising on tail vertebra); **la** left adrenal; **lint** large intestine; **lk** left kidney; **llg** left lung; **lt** left testis; **lv** liver; **mxt** maxillary teeth; **nv** non-vascular part of lung; **o** oesophagus; **ont** orbitonasal trough (opening of internal nostrils); **os** outer tongue sheath; **p** pancreas; **pp** primary palate; **ppt** teeth of palatine and pterygoid; **pt** posterior tongue; **re** rectum; **rlg** right lung; **sc** subcaudal scale; **sd** sperm duct; **sp** sperm groove; **sint** small intestine; **sn** spine; **sp** spleen; **st** stomach; **t** tongue; **thy** thyroid; **tlg** tracheal lung; **tm** thymus; **tr** trachea; **ur** ureter; **v** ventral scale (gastrostege).

muscles that change the shape of the lens to alter its focal length; there is a central area of the retina, the fovea, that gives greater definition; and screening against glare is achieved by the inclusion of yellow oil droplets in some of the cells of the retina to filter out excess light at the blue end of the spectrum. Most snakes have no muscles to change the shape of the lens and images are focussed by moving the lens bodily towards or away from the retina which, except in *Ahaetulla*, has no fovea.

In the few snakes known to be able to change the shape of the lens (e.g. *Natrix tessellata*) the mechanism for doing so is quite unlike that of lizards and if a light filter is present it is in the lens which is yellow. The eyes of snakes, even the best of them, are less perfect optical instruments than those of lizards and it seems possible that the ancestors of snakes may have been cryptozoic or burrowing creatures with reduced eyes; with changing habits, when eyes became important once again, the lost structures could not be re-acquired and other devices were developed instead.

Ears and tongue. The ears of snakes, also, are very different from those of most lizards. A typical lizard's ear consists of three essential parts, a membrane (tympanum) stretched across a tubular cavity that runs from the side of the head to the pharynx, a delicate bony rod (stapes) that connects the tympanum with the inner ear, and the inner ear itself (cochlea, etc.) which is embedded in the side of the skull. Snakes have an inner ear and a stapes but lack any trace of a tympanum or the cavities (auditory meatus, tympanic cavity and Eustachian tube) associated with it. Comparable degeneration of the ear is found in some families of burrowing lizards, but there is no complete linkage with this mode of life because some arboreal lizards, chameleons amongst them, have no tympanum.

Another and very characteristic feature of snakes, but one that is shared by some lizard families (e.g. monitors and tejus), is their tongue, which has a slender Y-shaped terminal portion that telescopes into a basal sheath (fig. 10). This may be an adjunct to yet another, and very important, sense organ, Jacobson's organ, which is described on p. 28.

The skull. The skull differences between lizards and snakes are principally concerned with their different methods of feeding. Most lizards have comparatively large, broad heads with correspondingly capacious mouths that have strong, rigid jaws, capable of biting and chewing food. Their whole skull forms a fairly rigid framework in which the following features are especially important. (fig. 11)

First, in the mid line there is an interorbital septum consisting of membrane and little struts of cartilage. Secondly, the roof of the mouth, and especially its hind part, is constructed to resist vertical pressure when food is being chewed and swallowed; the bones of this region – the pterygoids – are

22

Fig. 10. Head of *Boa constrictor*. Note the Y-shaped terminal portion of the tongue.
Photo: British Museum (Natural History): courtesy Zoological Society of London

firmly attached to the upper jaw and palate in front and to the quadrate behind and in between they are supported by both vertical struts (epipterygoid bones and lateral buttresses (basipterygoid processes). Finally, the two halves of the lower jaw are firmly united to form a largely inflexible 'U'.

Snakes, on the other hand, do not have teeth suitable for cutting up food into smaller pieces as some lizards do and swallow it whole. Since they have relatively narrow heads and small mouths this might be expected to restrict them to a diet of small creatures that would have to be very abundant; but this handicap has been avoided in almost all of them by the development of an enormously distensible and elastic mouth.

The bones composing the upper and lower jaws are loosely connected, instead of being rigidly united to each other and to the cranium, so that the whole circumference of the mouth is flexible and distensible. An interorbital septum occurs in the majority of snakes but its structure is unlike that of lizards. The bones of the snout have a movable articulation with the braincase which may allow the snout to be raised, thus increasing the gape, whilst at the hind end of the skull other changes have taken place which permit the width of the mouth

23

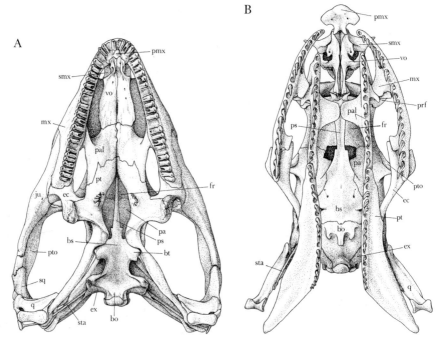

B

A

Fig. 11. Palatal views of a lizard and a snake. A. An iguanid lizard *(Cyclura carinata)*. B. A colubrid snake *(Ptyas mucosus)*. Key to abbreviations p. 7.

to be increased temporarily during swallowing. The upper temporal arcade has vanished, with loss of the jugal bone, and the pterygoids have not only lost their vertical and lateral supports (epipterygoids and basipterygoid processes) but are flexibly attached to the lower ends of the quadrates, and are consequently mobile on the rest of the skull.

This mobility has two important sequels. In the first place the lower end of the quadrate, being no longer firmly anchored, is much more free to swing backwards, forwards or sideways, thus facilitating retraction and protraction of the jaws of that side whilst lateral movement increases the width of the angles of the mouth, by muscles connecting the braincase with the palatine and pterygoid (fig. 14). The other sequel is that, since the roof of the mouth is no longer strutted away from the cranium, there would be risk of damage to the lower surface of the brain when a struggling victim was being swallowed. This danger has, however, been averted because the bones that roof the cranium (frontals and parietals) have grown downwards on either side of the brain to enclose it completely in a bony capsule.

24

TABLE 3

Some differences between the suborders of Squamata

	amphisbaenians	lizards	snakes
1 Forelimbs and shoulder girdle	vest.(+)	+ (vest.)	−
2 Hindlimbs and/or pelvis	vest.(−)	+	−(+)
3 Upper temporal arcade	−	+ (−)	−
4 Jugal bone	−(+)	+ (−)	−
5 Interorbital septum	−	+ (−)	−(+)
6 Brain totally enclosed in bony capsule	+ (almost)	−	+
7 Bones of upper jaw and snout suturally united	+	+	−(+?)
8 Supratemporal bone movable	vest.(−)	−	+ (−)
9 Epipterygoid bones	−(vest.)	+ (−)	−
10 Basipterygoid processes	+	+ (−)	−(+)
11 Pineal foramen	−	+ (−)	−
12 Mandibular rami suturally united	+	+ (−)	−
13 Zygantra and zygosphenes	−	−(+)	+
14 Caudal vertebrae with cleavage planes	−(+)	+ (−)	−(+)
15 Bronchial lungs	1(l)(2)	2 1(r)	1(r)(2)
16 Tracheal lung	−	−	−(+)
17 Urinary bladder	−	+ (−)	−
18 Gastrosteges	−	−	+ (−)
19 Rectus superficialis muscles	+	+ (−)	+
20 Movable eyelids	−	+ (−)	−
21 Nictitating membrane	−	+ (−)	−
22 Scleral ossicles	−(+)	+ (−)	−
23 Ciliary muscles for visual accommodation	−	+ (−)	−
24 Fovea centralis	−	+ (−)	−(+)
25 Tympanum, tympanic cavity and Eustachian tubes	−	+ (−)	−
26 Two very long pointed tips on the tongue	+	−(+)	+(−)
27 Osteoderms beneath scales	−	+ (−)	−

Where snakes are variable the rarer condition is normal for lizards.　　vest. = vestigial.
Symbols + and − indicate presence or absence and where both appear the condition shown first is the more usual.

Changes in the lower jaw are less extensive but equally important, the most vital being the development of a highly elastic ligament connecting its two halves (rami) at the chin; this ligament permits considerable independent movement of each ramus and also allows them to be pushed widely apart when bulky objects are being swallowed.

The tail vertebrae. While many lizards and some amphisbaenians have special cleavage planes in their tail vertebrae, a similar structure and mechanism in snakes seems to be confined to two genera (*Pliocercus* and *Scaphiodontophis*). Neither the snakes nor the amphisbaenians can regrow their tails, an inability that contrasts with the well-known regenerative powers of some lizards.

The affinities of snakes and lizards

It is clear that there are numerous differences between typical lizards and typical snakes (see Table 3), but there are very few characters that distinguish the two groups absolutely. Some lizards that have taken an evolutionary path parallel with that of the snakes, in, for example, loss of limbs, have naturally acquired one or more snake-like characters, and conversely, a minority of snakes retain as an ancestral inheritance lizard-like features that the majority have lost. The two groups are obviously very closely akin and there can be little doubt that the snakes are an off-shoot from some lizard-like stock. The environmental conditions in which a terrestrial animal would secure an advantage by developing a serpentine form and method of locomotion are to be found in very dense herbage or in loose soil where burrowing is possible without excavation. These environments, and especially the first-mentioned, give concealment and protection from enemies that do not have equally good, or better, tunnelling powers, and at the same time they offer to a predator a varied food supply of other creatures seeking their sanctuary. It is, therefore, reasonable to look for the ancestors of snakes in some group of lizard-like reptiles that possessed potentialities for burrowing.

While the general affinities of snakes and lizards are not in doubt the precise affinities are. One view is that the nearest living relatives of snakes are the varanoid lizards—the Platynota, which is composed of monitors (Varanidae), Gila monsters (Helodermatidae) and the rare Bornean *Lanthanotus* together with the extinct mosasaurs, aigialosaurs and dolichosaurs.

An alternative view is that snakes diverged from early lizard stock before the appearance of any of the modern lizard groups. But these views are conjectural, because direct evidence of the precise origin of snakes has so far eluded the palaeontologists.

3 *The senses of snakes*

Since an animal's powers of perception form a vital link in determining how it reacts to the world around it, the modified sense organs of snakes must influence their behaviour and, perhaps, place limitations on the types of environment in which they can live.

Sight

Amongst the peculiarities of their eyes mentioned in the previous chapter, probably the most important are the focussing arrangements and the absence of a retinal fovea in all except one genus. A fixed-focus lens that has to be moved bodily to give visual accommodation may be expected to be effective only over a limited range when the eye itself is not enlarged to provide a greater space for its movement; and the lack of a fovea – the area that is designed to give greater definition – must result in poor perception of detail. On the other hand, the whole of the retina is, like that in the human peripheral field of vision, very perceptive of movement. So, with their eyes directed laterally and thus giving a very wide field of view, snakes may be expected to have a correspondingly wide visual field in which the slightest movement will be recorded but which lacks acuity; this is confirmed by their behaviour. However, while perception of movement seems to be important to some snakes, the majority rely more on their olfactory senses with which they can detect dead and other immobile prey such as eggs (pp. 36 and 75).

A number of large-eyed terrestrial and arboreal snakes may have binocular vision, but a fovea has been reported only in the Oriental whip snakes (*Ahaetulla*) (Plate 9). These and the African twig snakes (*Thelotornis*) have large and prominent eyes with slit-like horizontal pupils which are so long that light from directly in front of the snout, or even from the opposite side, can enter at the anterior corner and produce an image on the outer edge of the posterior quadrant of the retina where there is a fovea or fovea-like area.

Hearing

The absence of an ear drum must obviously affect the auditory sense, because this structure has the function of collecting air-borne sound waves and transmitting them through a bony rod (the stapes) to the inner ear, where they are translated into nerve impulses that reach the brain via the auditory nerve. Experiments show that snakes cannot perceive most air-borne sounds although they do respond to a restricted range of low frequency waves and to vibrations of the surface on which they rest. These vibrations arise from the movements of other animals or inanimate objects disturbed by wind and water and so forth. They are picked up, at least partly, by the jawbones and transmitted to the quadrate bone and thence to the stapes, which is in close contact with it. Recent research suggests that the lung may also be involved in the transmission of sound and other vibrations.

Smell and Jacobson's organ

Sight, hearing and smell are the main distant senses and although the first two are indifferent or poor in snakes, an accessory organ, called Jacobson's organ, enables them to follow a scent trail. It consists of a pair of saccular structures that lie embedded in the anterior part of the palate; each sac, which is lined with sensory epithelium, communicates with the mouth by a short duct. When a snake is active the tongue is in almost constant motion, being alternately protruded, with its tips flickering, and withdrawn. When it is withdrawn, any particles picked up by the snake's tongue from the air or from objects that have been investigated, are transferred to the sensory lining of Jacobson's organ which communicates with the brain by a special branch of the olfactory nerve. The means by which the particles are passed by the tongue to the ducts is uncertain, but it is possible that the tips are inserted directly into the ducts. The sensations recorded are almost certainly akin to, if not identical with, the sense of smell, and the constant use of the tongue by snakes is an indication of the reliance placed on this sense.

The other senses

The modification of the tongue for use with Jacobson's organ has, however, probably resulted in some loss of the sense of taste, for there are few taste buds on it; but the remaining senses, none of which is concerned with the perception of distant events, are all acute. The sense of balance, which arises partly from the semicircular canals that respond to movements of the head, and partly from the muscles that are subjected to changing gravitational stresses when other parts of the animal are tilted, is especially good; witness the ability of climbing snakes to move freely along slender swaying branches or to rest on a fence wire. And their sense of touch is not inferior; diminutive tubercles on the convex parts

28

of the head, especially on the snout and chin, less commonly on the belly and less commonly still on the trunk and tail, seem to have a tactile function.

On the back, flanks and tail, and sometimes also on the head, there occur minute circular areas, barely visible to the naked eye, where the keratinous layer of the skin is much thinner and where the underlying epidermis is richly provided with bundles of nerve fibres. These 'apical pits' may be heat receptors, because a sensitive mechanism to detect variations in the amount of heat radiation to which they are exposed is essential to 'cold-blooded' animals. All snakes, whether possessing apical pits or not, are certainly acutely sensitive to temperature changes in their environment and to infra-red radiation, whilst some boas and pythons (Chap. 9), and all pit vipers (Chap. 12), have special heat receptor organs that enable them to locate warm-blooded prey, with accuracy, in the dark.

4 Snakes and their environments

Temperature regulation

In 'warm-blooded' animals (birds and mammals) the temperature of the body is controlled at a constant, or nearly constant, level. When the external temperature falls below this level the amount of heat they lose by radiation and conduction is minimized by their insulating layer of fur, hair, blubber or feathers and the small amount lost is made good by the heat generated in their tissues. When, on the other hand, they receive too much heat from their surroundings their body temperature is prevented from rising by an increase in the rate of evaporation of moisture from their respiratory surfaces as a result of panting and also, in many cases, by increased sweating.

The 'cold-blooded' reptiles generate far less heat and lose it far more readily because they have no heat-insulating layer and the losses sustained are often too great to be compensated by metabolic heat, at least under resting conditions; and, when the external temperature rises they are equally unable to control their body temperature by physiological means because they lack sweat glands and the control they can achieve by panting is limited.

Nevertheless their tissues are not especially tolerant and, merely to survive, snakes must maintain their body temperature within the temperature range of about 4–38°C regardless of climatic conditions; at temperatures below 2–4°C they become completely torpid and at 38–47°C (depending on the species and the duration of the exposure), some of the proteins in their tissues undergo irreversible chemical changes that cause death. The optimum temperature range within which they can achieve full activity is more narrowly circumscribed still and the average limits for most species lie between about 21 and 37°C.

In the absence of structural and physiological regulators, temperature control is achieved by behaviour, and the habits of snakes differ considerably according to the climatic conditions. In the tropics, for example, where there is no winter season in which the air temperature remains constantly below their activity level, there is no period of winter torpor and the principal hazard is the midday sun. Under these conditions species with nocturnal or burrowing habits have

30

an advantage and diurnal species tend to operate in the shade or they become crepuscular, remaining under cover during the heat of the day; and at the peak of the hot season they may remain inactive for longer periods when they are said to be aestivating.

In higher latitudes and at higher altitudes the snakes face different problems, one of the most acute being the winter when the temperature of their surroundings may remain below their activity level for several months. Survival through this season is only possible if a frost-free underground refuge for hibernation can be found and this is the factor that determines the geographical and topographical limits of snakes. None can survive where the subsoil remains frozen throughout the year, as it does in the polar regions and on high mountains even in the tropics. Very few species do, in fact, approach this limit at all closely, but the Adder crosses the arctic circle, reaching 68°N latitude in Scandinavia, and the Common garter snake ranges to about 67°N in the Yukon; no snakes occur in Antarctica or on any of the subantarctic islands and the most southerly record is in the province of Santa Cruz, Argentina, where a pit viper (*Bothrops ammodytoides*) has been found. Some of the montane limits are 3000 metres in the Swiss Alps (the Adder) and the mountains of New Guinea (Boelen's python), 4400 metres in Mexico (Mexican dusky rattlesnake) and 4900 metres in the Himalayas (Himalayan pit viper).

During aestivation snakes are inactive from choice and are merely avoiding unfavourable conditions; but during hibernation they are in a state of physiological torpor directly produced by a low temperature and so long as this persists they are helpless. It follows, therefore, that the place of refuge must be found before torpor develops and that its choice is vitally important; should it prove not to be frost-free there is no possibility of making a change.

When the midday temperatures in autumn begin to fall until they scarcely exceed the activity level a migratory tendency may develop. When, for example, the maximum shade temperature drops to about 10°C (in early October in Britain) Adders begin to move towards sheltered spots on south-facing slopes where they bask when the sun shines and creep into natural crannies or the burrows of other creatures by night. As the season advances their visits to the surface become progressively shorter and finally cease until the midday temperature again rises to an average of 8°C. In Britain this normally occurs in late February or early March, and the average length of hibernation is around 135 days. But the duration of this inactive period will clearly vary not only with vagaries of the seasons but from place to place according to topographical and geographical climatic differences; in the case of the Adder it varies from about 105 days in southern Europe to 275 days in the far north. Differences of this magnitude in the active life of a snake, from 8·5 months per annum to about 3, have profound effects, because to secure all the food necessary for

31

growth, reproduction and winter reserves in about a third of the time is impossible. So growth is slower and, what is more important, the reproductive cycle is prolonged so that young are produced only every other year instead of annually.

In addition to the hazards of colder winters, increasing distance from the tropics affects the snake fauna through the general lowering of the average temperature even in summer. As the number of nights on which the temperature remains above 21°C diminishes, nocturnal species become progressively more handicapped until they can no longer survive unless, as some do, they change their habits; the Adder, for instance, is often crepuscular or nocturnal in the south of its range but much more diurnal in the extreme north. And species adapted for a truly subterranean life will obviously not be able to exist in regions where the underground temperature never reaches the minimum they need for full activity. So, in the cooler parts of the temperate zones, and at high altitudes nearer the equator, surface-dwelling, diurnal species predominate and the daily cycle of temperature variation affects even these.

In spring and autumn, especially, the shade temperature of the air may not reach the activity level except during the middle of the day. But snakes can raise their body temperature above the air temperature by basking in the sun, and the rate at which this rise takes place depends not only on the intensity of the solar radiation but also on the animals' size and colour. Smaller forms have less mass to heat as well as having, proportionally, a greater surface area in relation to their mass. Consequently they will warm up to the requisite temperature more readily than larger species, and thus secure the advantage of longer periods of activity in cool but sunny weather. So, the snakes of the colder regions are almost all of small size and it is not uncommon to find that where a species has a wide altitudinal range it is represented at higher altitudes by dwarf races which may also be darker in colour, sometimes almost black, because this type of colour reflects less, and absorbs more, of the sun's rays.

Many lizards are able to change their colour, not only in response to changes in external conditions (e.g. temperature, light intensity, background colour) but also in response to emotion (anger, fear, etc.). These colour changes are thought to be controlled by the nervous system and by hormones produced by the pituitary and adrenal glands. Few snakes, however, have any powers of colour-change and where it does occur the magnitude of the changes is very slight indeed. Their skin pigments are of greater consequence in relation to their animate than their inanimate environment, and mainly connected with defence and concealment.

The skin – boundary between body and environment

The skin itself is a snake's main protection against a number of physical hazards, such as mechanical injury, desiccation and so forth, and its methods of locomotion subject it to a great deal of friction that is not localized at a few points, as it is in animals that have limbs.

Fig. 12. A sloughed snake's skin. Beginning at the lips, the old outer layer of skin, including the eye coverings, is periodically shed.
Photo: Nathan W. Cohen

The whole of the horny epidermis has to be renewed periodically, partly to compensate for wear and partly to allow for growth. Of the three layers which compose the skin, the innermost is the thickest and in it the pigment cells are situated whilst the middle layer is very thin and consists of cells that are continually growing and dividing in a plane parallel with the surface. The new cells produced in this way die and become converted into a continuous sheet of horny material (keratin) which forms the third layer that covers the whole of the body.

Production of this horny epidermis does not proceed at an unchecked uniform rate, but from time to time a film of exudate is produced and this separates its older (and outer) layers from the younger ones beneath them. When this occurs the whole of the skin acquires an opaque, milky appearance and even the eye-covering is affected so that the snake becomes partially blind and usually

33

goes into hiding. After some days, however, the eye clears again and four or five days later the old epidermis is sloughed in one piece. Moulting begins along the lips, the old 'skin' being turned back on itself by the snake rubbing the sides of its head on the ground, and then the body muscles contract in shivering waves that loosen it still more; further rubbing turns it back over the head and then the snake crawls out of it, turning it inside out in doing so (fig. 12).

Young snakes moult soon after they are born (or hatch), and in the first year of life when growth is most rapid, there may be up to seven moults, or even more. In subsequent years the skin is usually shed soon after emergence from hibernation, but the frequency of moulting diminishes as age increases and the growth rate gets less.

Life in the desert

Although not as impervious to water as has often been supposed, the reptilian skin nevertheless plays an important part in water conservation. The rate at which water is lost through the skin is linked with the snake's environment, being highest in aquatic species and lowest in those that live in very arid conditions. Another factor that renders snakes adaptable to living in deserts is their ability to excrete nitrogenous waste in a semi-solid state.

Apart from the perils of very high temperatures and water scarcity certain types of desert present difficulties for snakes in connection with their normal undulatory method of locomotion which, as previously mentioned, depends upon the existence of fixed resistance points against which the body waves can exert their pressure. Very loose shifting sand, with little or no vegetation, provides inadequate 'footholds' and several different kinds of snakes have, in different places, developed a modified form of progression, known as 'sidewinding', in which they take a succession of steps over the surface instead of slithering; the thrust at each step is directed obliquely downwards instead of tangentially to the surface. The best known exponents of this type of locomotion are mostly vipers (Plate 14) such as the cerastes vipers and carpet vipers (Plate 15) of the desert belt from the Sahara to Sind, the Sidewinder, a rattlesnake of the North American desert areas, and some puff adders in southern Africa (Plate 15). As in normal undulatory serpentine locomotion, side to side waves originate anteriorly and travel backwards along the body, but each has a slight vertical curvature that lifts the body clear of the surface as the snake transfers its weight from one position to the next; stages in sidewinding are shown diagrammatically in fig. 8.

To escape from the intense midday heat a desert snake must be able to bury itself. Some of them, like the sand boas (Plate 4) and the awl-headed snakes (*Lytorhynchus*), do this by burrowing into the sand head first, but others, such as the carpet and cerastes vipers, have a different method of burying themselves.
34

The body is flattened by spreading the ribs outwards and becomes almost triangular in section with the lower flanks forming an angular ridge along each side. Writhing movements cause these ridges to dig into the loose surface and the snake sinks vertically downwards as the soil is displaced over its back. Frequently, however, the upper surface of the head is left exposed for breathing, and it is not unusual for the nostrils to be provided with valves to exclude sand when, in an emergency, the head has to be withdrawn below the surface (e.g. *Eristicophis*).

Life in the water

Vertically directed, valvular nostrils are also commonly found in aquatic snakes to enable them to breathe at the surface, but to exclude water when they are submerged; and various groups that have adopted this mode of life have acquired different devices for closing the nasal passages (see wart snakes, Chap. 9; homalopsines, Chap. 10; sea snakes, Chap. 11).

Water as an environmental medium naturally calls for other adaptive structures and behaviour, but in snakes these are much less extensive than in other air-breathing vertebrates. Fully aquatic species cannot, of course, maintain their body temperature above that of their surroundings by basking and so they are restricted to tropical waters; eggs of reptiles cannot develop in water so reproduction must be viviparous (Chap. 7); and locomotion makes different demands, though these are surprisingly slight.

The majority of aquatic snakes live in shallow waters and spend much of their time moving over the bottom where the normal terrestrial methods of locomotion serve equally well. It is only for swimming away from the bottom that modifications are needed and even here the basic principles of undulatory 'serpentine' locomotion apply. Despite the absence of fixed resistance points, the normal body waves in their passage from head to tail encounter resistance from the water and some of this is displaced backwards; the result is a forward thrust proportional to the mass of water moved and the rate at which it is set in motion. Obviously a cylindrical rod, a snake's normal body shape, is not a good instrument for moving water and a flattened blade is much more effective; so, although all snakes can swim, and often surprisingly well, the more specialized aquatic types have bodies with some degree of side to side flattening and tails that may be completely paddle-like.

5 Nutrition

Diet

As mentioned in a previous chapter snakes, none of which has grinding teeth, have to swallow their prey whole; and there are no vegetarians* and very few carrion feeders amongst them. The majority can track down inactive prey by using their sense of smell, but a few that depend more heavily on their visual powers will only attempt to eat prey that has been seen to move and is of an appropriate size.

Reticulated pythons of 5–10 metres have been reported as having suffocated and swallowed human beings, but only one such case is well documented and apparently reliable. The incident occurred during daylight on the remote island of Salibathu, north of the Celebes, S.E. Asia, and the victim was a fourteen-year-old boy. When the snake was found two days after it had eaten its gargantuan meal it was killed; the boy's body was extracted covered with the snake's digestive juices but with seemingly little breakdown of human tissue. The accounts of large pythons or boas eating 'fully grown' pigs or deer can be misleading by failing to specify the species of deer or type of pig involved. A 4-metre African rock python (Plate 3) is accurately reported to have eaten a half grown sitatunga that weighed about 27 kg. The very experienced game warden who recorded this case came to the conclusion that a 9-metre snake of this species (one of the largest known) would not be able to cope with an antelope of much more than about 68 kg.

Although many of the larger snakes may have a varied diet, and one that changes with age as their increasing size enables them to overpower and eat larger creatures, the majority have limited food preferences. Some feed exclusively on frogs, others on lizards and yet others on small rodents. Among the more unusual specialist feeders are egg-eaters (*Dasypeltinae*), snail eaters (*Pareinae* and *Dipsadinae*), fish-egg-eaters (some sea snakes), crab-eaters (*Fordonia*) and termite-eaters (*Leptotyphlops*) whilst a surprisingly large number have a diet consisting almost exclusively of other snakes; in a few instances the preferred food may consist of only a single abundant species, but such narrow specialization is unusual.

*Vegetable matter may be swallowed accidentally and there are a few records of egg-eating snakes and pythons having eaten fruit.

Capturing and consuming their prey

To find food, nocturnal snakes prowl in suitable places; but many diurnal species, especially those that are well camouflaged, lurk rather than prowl, relying on their colour and posture to escape observation until a potential victim comes close enough to be struck by a sudden lunge.

Fig. 13. The tentacles of the Fishing snake *(Erpeton tentaculum)*.
Photo: Nathan W. Cohen

There are also a few species that attract their prey by displaying a lure. For example, several pit vipers of the genus *Agkistrodon*, including the American copperhead, the Mexican cantil and the Oriental Hump-nosed viper, have yellow or reddish tails that contrast sharply with their otherwise dull inconspicuous colours. When they are lying coiled and at rest the tail is hidden beneath the body, but if a lizard or frog approaches the tail is raised vertically and wriggled, simulating a worm or caterpillar. And the African twig snake, which, as its name implies, looks like an innocuous branch when not moving, is said to use its brilliantly coloured orange-red tongue in the same way. The two scaly tentacles on the tip of the snout of the aquatic Fishing snake (fig. 13) were at one time believed to act as a lure, but although they have been found to possess a rich network of nerves and blood vessels a sensory function has not been demonstrated and they may merely increase the effectiveness of the snake's camouflage.

37

The lunging strike of a snake is often delivered with great speed; a Prairie rattle-snake's strike, for example, has been timed and found to be between 1·6 and 3·5 metres per second which, although not as fast as a man can strike with his fist, will seldom fail. If the strike is successful and the teeth have secured a grip, most non-venomous snakes begin swallowing almost at once, after some preliminary gulping movements to obtain a firmer hold or to shift the grip to the victim's head. The process of engulfing the meal depends upon the mobility of the bones of the upper jaw, the elasticity of the ligament connecting the two halves of the lower jaw and the shape of the teeth, which are thorn-like and slightly curved with their points directed obliquely backwards; normally there are two rows of teeth on the palate (palatine and pterygoid bones) in addition to the rows along the jaws themselves. Whilst the snake maintains a firm grip with the jaws on one side of the mouth, it relaxes its grip with the opposite side and pushes this a short distance forwards, the teeth disengaging in the process. By doing this first with one side of the mouth and then the other, and by the upper and lower jaws working alternately, the snake forcibly pulls the meal into its mouth which is stretched in the process; the lower ends of the quadrate bones are pushed sideways and the halves of the lower jaw forced apart whilst the ligament connecting them is stretched and distorted to the shape of the prey.

Unless the victim is quite small, when a gulp or two will dispose of it, the time taken to swallow a meal may be considerable, up to an hour or more, and during this period, with the mouth and throat filled to capacity, the snake would be in danger of suffocation. This danger is circumvented by a special modification which allows the glottis (the opening of the windpipe) to be protruded and retracted. When a bulky meal is being swallowed the glottis is pushed forwards over the tongue so that it projects beyond the mouth and breathing is un-impeded, because the windpipe, like that of all other vertebrates, is reinforced with rings of cartilage that prevent it from collapsing under pressure.

Subjugation – constriction and venom

Although most invertebrates and the smaller and weaker vertebrates can be swallowed without great difficulty, larger and more active animals need subjugation and for this two methods are employed, constriction and venom. Many snakes, including the European smooth snake, hold their struggling victims by throwing one or two coils of their body around them, and this grip is maintained until deglutition is well advanced. The Elephant-trunk snake uses a combination of constriction and its loose folds of coarse sandpaper-like skin to trap fish. From this it is only a short step to true constriction which is practised by a great many other snakes of several different families, including the boids. Here a greater number of coils is thrown round the prey and the victim, if it breathes by lungs, is suffocated. As soon as it is insensible or dead it is released, re-examined by the tongue and then swallowed. The swallowing reaction, though

38

largely automatic once it has begun, can be reversed if the snake is disturbed and the meal will be regurgitated. It is the appearance of such rejected prey, mangled by the jaws and teeth and covered in saliva and mucus from the mouth and throat, that has given rise to the erroneous belief that a constricting snake crushes its victim into a sausage-like shape and covers it with slime for ease of swallowing.

Venom that can be injected to produce paralysis or death has been evolved several times in the animal kingdom, in, for example, coelenterates, echinoderms, molluscs, insects, arachnids and fishes as well as snakes. The origin of the venom and the method of injecting it varies in the different groups of snakes. In most colubrids it is the product of Duvernoy's gland and it drains onto the teeth of the upper jaw. The venomous snakes of the families Elapidae and Viperidae lack this gland but have a venom gland which, while it also lies along the side of the head, as Duvernoy's gland does, may also extend far back along the body in some forms; its contents are injected into the victim by the specially modified fangs at the front of the upper jaw.

The saliva of snakes is a digestive juice that contains, amongst other things, substances whose function is to bring about a chemical breakdown of complex organic materials in the food to simpler compounds that are soluble and can be absorbed in solution through the walls of the intestine. So, injection of the secretion of even a 'harmless' snake will produce at least local damage to the tissues of its prey; but the amount that can enter through the small punctures made by the simple needle-like teeth typical of most snakes is so minute that the damage is usually negligible. Nevertheless toxic effects are occasionally known to follow the bites of snakes with simple teeth. For instance, the Pinewoods snake of the southeastern United States, which preys on frogs, does not begin swallowing its meal immediately after it has caught it as most harmless non-constricting snakes do; instead it holds its victims in its jaws until they are insensible before beginning to eat them. The Japanese Yamakagashi, whose posterior maxillary teeth are enlarged but grooveless, is a dangerously venomous species.

To produce a more effective means of rapidly subduing large and powerful prey it is clearly necessary to elaborate more rapidly acting 'venom' and to have a means of injecting larger doses of it, preferably deep into the bloodstream so that it will be swiftly carried to other parts of the body and produce general effects. The first, and least efficient, stage of such a device is found in the 'opisthoglyphous' colubrine snakes (Chap. 10) in which a few teeth (2–5) at the hind end of the upper jaw (where the duct from Duvernoy's gland discharges) are more or less enlarged and have a groove running from base to tip on their outer surface. These grooves provide a channel by which the venom squeezed out of Duvernoy's gland can enter the fang punctures; but because an open groove functions by capillary action and the liquid is not injected under pressure, few of these back-fanged snakes are dangerous to human beings though there are exceptions (see Chap. 10).

A more efficient system is found in the front-fanged (proteroglyphous) snakes – the cobras, kraits, mambas, coral snakes, sea snakes, etc. (Chap. 11), where there are two fangs situated in a more advantageous position at the front of the upper jaw. These fangs are perforated from base to tip like a hypodermic needle, the perforation having evolved from an open groove by the overgrowth of its lips until they have met. There is thus an enclosed canal opening near the tip of the tooth and its base, and the duct from the venom gland is closely applied to the basal opening.

An even more efficient apparatus is found in *Atractaspis* (p. 79) and in vipers where similar fangs are present but are very much longer and so capable of injecting the venom more deeply. A very long fixed fang could not be accommodated inside the mouth and the mole vipers and the viperids have evolved an erectile fang that lies flat when the mouth is closed (figs. 14 and 27). The erection is achieved, not by the development of a hinge where the tooth is attached to the jawbone, but by an arrangement that allows the bone itself to rotate through an angle of nearly 90 degrees in the vertical plane. The maxillary bone is very short, shorter than deep, with no teeth except the fangs and the rotary movement is produced by muscles that slide the palatal bones (palatine and pterygoid) backwards and forwards. As the palatal bones slide, the movement is transmitted by a bony link (ectopterygoid bone) to the lower edge of the maxilla which, being so very short and deep, rolls instead of slides; when the palatal bones slide forwards the rolling movement erects the fangs from a position parallel with the roof of the mouth and the reverse movement folds them flat again.

Obviously the fangs can only be erected when the mouth is open, but the widely held belief that opening the mouth automatically erects the fangs is incorrect; the two actions frequently occur simultaneously, but a viper may sometimes be seen to yawn without moving its fangs at all or it may, in the middle of a yawn, erect them and fold them several times before closing its mouth.

Very many different chemical compounds have been identified in the toxic secretion of venomous snakes and the venom of any single species is a complex mixture. The substances can, however, be grouped into a limited number of

Fig. 14. Fang erection in the Puff adder *(Bitis arietans)*. A. Fang in retracted position. Superficial jaw muscles and venom gland exposed. B–C. Anterior and posterior views of maxilla. D. Fang erected, showing upper jawbones protracted by the deep muscles (prpt and levpt) and the maxilla and prefrontal rotated dorsally around their articulations with the prefrontal and frontal respectively. Fang retraction is accomplished primarily by the retractor muscle (rpt).
c major compressor muscle of vgl; **dm** depressor mandibulae; **ge** groove for articulation with ectopterygoid; **levpt** levator muscle of pterygoid; **lo** lower orifice of hollow fang; **prpt** protractor muscle of pterygoid; **rpt** retractor muscle of pterygoid; **uo** upper orifice of hollow fang; **vd** venom duct leading to uo; **vgl** venom gland. Key to other abbreviations p. 7.

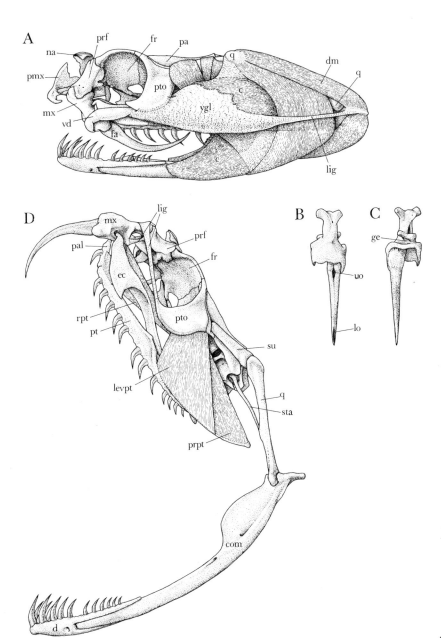

41

categories according to their effects. At the risk of over-simplification, four such groups may be considered, thus:

1. Substances that cause disintegration of the tissues, including the blood corpuscles and the linings of the blood vessels (cytolysins, haemorrhagins, haemolysins, etc.).
2. Anticoagulants that destroy the clotting power of the blood and result in profuse bleeding especially when the substances of group 1 are present.
3. Coagulants that increase the clotting power of the blood and produce thromboses.
4. Poisons that act on the nervous system (neurotoxins), especially the motor nerves of the respiratory system and the heart.

Most venoms contain substances of all four of these groups, as well as an enzyme (hyaluronidase) that causes their rapid diffusion through the tissues; and, because the properties of some of them are antagonistic, it is clear that the effects of a bite will depend to a very large extent, upon the proportions in which each occurs.

In very general terms (and there are many exceptions) haemorrhagic substances tend to predominate in viperid venoms and neurotoxins in the cobras and their allies. But each species has its own characteristic combination, though there may be considerable variation within a species especially in geographically wide-ranging forms; for example the venom of Prairie rattlesnakes living in the Great Plains has been found to be more than three times as toxic to mice as that from another race of the same species which lives in California. And even though the components and their relative proportions may be approximately the same there can be considerable differences in the total concentration in different individuals, depending upon age, sex, season and the time that has elapsed since the last bite.

The range of variation in the nature of snake venom is paralleled by the degree of tolerance shown by different animals, even to the same venom. Rabbits, for instance, are twice as susceptible to the venom of the Indian cobra as dogs which, in turn, are twenty-five times more susceptible than the Asiatic mongoose; cats are ten or twenty times as resistant to Australian black snake venom as monkeys of comparable size; and rats can tolerate six times as much Eastern diamond-back rattlesnake poison as guinea-pigs; and so on. This dual variability in venom toxicity and immunity, apart from making it quite impossible to produce a list of snakes in order of comparative virulence, has its effects on the lives of snakes in relation to their prey – it is clear that a snake will obtain an easier living if it concentrates on prey that is readily susceptible to its venom rather than on other animals that have some degree of natural resistance.

6 *Enemies and defence*

Enemies

Fig. 15. The death throes of a Hamadryad *(Ophiophagus hannah)* as it is strangled by the constricting coils of a reticulated python *(Python reticulatus)*. This encounter in the lowland rain forest of West Malaysia is unusual because the Hamadryad normally preys on other snakes, and pythons hunt warm blooded prey.
Photo: Peter Cockburn

Physiological immunity to the venom of forms which, like the Hamadryad (fig. 15) and the kraits, prey on other snakes, may give a few species some measure of protection, but more frequently it is the predators that have the immunity. The kingsnake of North America, for example, and the Mussurana of tropical America are both immune, or very resistant, to pit-viper venom and their diet includes such dangerous forms as copperheads, cottonmouths, rattlesnakes and the Fer-de-lance.

Other enemies of snakes also profit from some degree of immunity to certain types of snake venom, and amongst the better known of these are the Asiatic mongoose *(Herpestes)*, highly tolerant of Indian cobra venom; the South African meerkat *(Suricata)*, resistant to Cape cobra poison but susceptible to that of the Puff adder; the European hedgehog, thirty or forty times as resistant to adder venom as a guinea-pig; and a few New World skunks and opossums whose blood contains antibodies that can neutralize the venom of pit vipers.

The very numerous predatory enemies of snakes are, however, by no means limited to animals possessing some immunity and they include some terrapins as well as mammals such as pigs, dogs, foxes, badgers and coyotes, and various birds like golden, harrier and bateleur eagles, horned owls, red-tailed buzzards, road-runners, ground hornbills, secretary-birds, cariamas and chungas. The greatest enemy of all, however, is man because not only does he, through fear or prejudice, or to safeguard his domestic animals, wage an unremitting war on snakes, but his industrial and agricultural developments have an indirect effect that is infinitely more damaging; the balanced ecological conditions in which snakes find their essential requirements are irrevocably destroyed.

Defence

Against the wholesale destruction of their habitats individual snakes have no defence; only the adaptable species can survive. But against predators they have defensive reactions and devices many of which are basically the same as those used in obtaining food. Almost invariably the first reaction to the presence of a suspected enemy is to try to escape observation either by remaining motionless or by withdrawing under cover. If this manoeuvre fails it is usually followed by visual and auditory warnings, or by the use of chemical deterrents, and in the last resort by an attack using the same techniques that are used in securing and subduing prey. The same sequence of defence reactions is not always employed, nor yet the full sequence, so that even when the behaviour pattern of a species is known, individuals influenced by the conditions of the moment may behave quite unpredictably. A snake taken by surprise, for instance, or one that has already been disturbed, is much more likely to be immediately aggressive without warning, whilst hunger and the mating season are also amongst the factors that may lead to apparently unprovoked attacks.

Concealment by colour, structure and posture
Colour and pattern, shape and posture, all play their parts as aids to concealment and although snakes are unable to change their colour to harmonize with the background most of them have some form of procrypsis or camouflage. Two main types of concealing coloration may be recognized, one (procryptic) in which the colour and pattern closely resemble those of the background, and the other (disruptive) where the arrangement and distribution of the colours

44

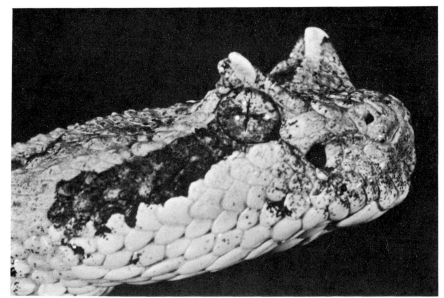

Fig. 16. The Sidewinder *(Crotalus cerastes)*, showing horns above the eyes, and large sensory pit between eye and nostril. The pit is sensitive to temperature changes and helps the snake locate its prey.
Photo: Nathan W. Cohen

distracts the observer's eye so that the shape of the animal is lost. Examples of the former are found among the arboreal snakes some of which are either a uniform leaf-green that matches the foliage or some shade of brownish-grey like the bark. Disruptive colours are less common and the two best known examples are the Gaboon viper and the River Jack, of the damp forests of tropical Africa, in both of which there are contrasting colours – purple, crimson, rose, pale blue, silver, yellow, russet and black – arranged in complex geometrical patterns.

Whilst colours that are purely procryptic or purely disruptive are not common, a great many snakes have some combination of the two. Thus tree snakes may be dappled to harmonize with highlights and shadows, or have darker bars that break up the outline, or both; or there may be longitudinal lines that so exaggerate the appearance of slenderness that the animal looks like a thin twig or the tendril of an epiphytic vine, whilst a dark bar that cuts through the eye and makes its circular outline less obvious is a very common feature. Desert species are usually pale in colour, grey or dun, with stippling like sand grains and darker blotches with indefinite margins, or a disruptive pattern of dark saddles or chevrons down the back; and so forth.

Cryptic and disruptive colours are also sometimes enhanced by structure and behaviour. Desert species, for instance, may have thorn-like spines above the

45

eyes (fig. 16) or on the end of the snout and these may disguise the outline of the head as they lie half buried in the sand. And some arboreal forms have even longer forwardly directed nasal projections that completely alter the silhouette of the head, whilst others, like the African vipers of the genus *Atheris*, normally rest with the forepart of the body raised and bent at a sharp angle so that, with their cryptic coloration, they look like kinked or half broken twigs.

Intimidation by display

Colour and behaviour may, however, serve defensively not by concealing, but by advertising, the snake's presence or by distracting attention. The sudden display of previously concealed markings and colours (Plate 7), causing surprised hesitation on the part of the enemy, is a common device in many groups of animals and in snakes it is often accompanied by a sudden change of shape or posture. Most of them, when alarmed, inflate themselves (Plate 11) and many also raise themselves off the ground as far as possible, as if preparing to launch an attack. The shape of the distended neck varies greatly, sometimes being no more than a general increase in diameter, but in other instances the swelling is localized. In some species it is globular, as in the case of the Guyana chickensnake, which looks as if it had just swallowed an egg (hence its name), but more frequently it is oval and flattened. No matter what its shape may be, however, there is one inevitable result; the increase in diameter exposes the skin between the scales and this is often not only different in colour but has a bold and distinctive pattern.

The markings on the 'hoods' of cobras (Plate 12) are familiar examples of patterns disclosed by separation of the neck scales (though in these snakes the neck expansion is brought about by rib movement and not by inflation) but other, less well-known, instances are equally striking, *e.g.* in the African twig snake, where the inflated neck is compressed from side-to-side, the exposed skin is startlingly white with transverse black bars and in the Oriental whip snake there are similar, but oblique, bars of black and white.

Although the striking colour-patterns thus suddenly displayed are intimidatory they are not 'warning colours' as usually understood since they depend for their effect on surprise and are not intimately linked with venomous species. A number of small and mainly cryptozoic members of the cobra family (Elapidae, Chap. 11), however, have a livery of warning colours, usually in the form of alternating rings of red, black, and yellow or white (Plate 6). Those known best are the coral snakes of the New World *(Micrurus, Micruroides)* but there are also so-called 'coral snakes' with similar but less striking colours and markings in Africa *(Elapsoidea, Aspidelaps)*, the Orient *(Calliophis)* and Australia *(Rhinelaps, Brachyurophis, etc.)*. All these are venomous, but in each of the countries where they occur, except Australia, there are several quite harmless species with essentially similar colours (Plate 6), and in some instances the re-

46

semblance is so close that a detailed examination is necessary to distinguish between the venomous species and their mimics.

So-called 'mimicry' of quite a different nature is associated with behaviour that diverts the attention of an enemy. In many burrowing and semi-burrowing forms the tail is very short and bluntly rounded at the tip so that it is not unlike the head in outline (e.g. Rubber boa Plate 7). This alone could confuse an aggressor, but colour and behaviour sometimes seem designed to increase the chances of the attack being directed at the non-vital tail, leaving the head free for a surprise counter-attack. In some thread snakes (Chap. 8) both head and tail have a very obvious white spot, and in the African *Chilorhinophis* this type of 'directive mark' coloration is even more marked, for whilst the upper surface of the body is yellowish with three narrow black longitudinal lines, both the head and the short blunt tail are jet black, sometimes with a few lighter spots.

The greatest distraction to the attacker, however, is produced when a brightly coloured tail is used in the same way as for luring prey. The best known examples of this type of behaviour, sometimes called 'head mimicry', are found in the Malaysian banded coral snake and the Malaysian pipe snake. The former, a venomous species, when moving above ground sometimes carries its tail erect, thus exposing the under surface which is bright red, and, in the event of an alarm, the raised tail makes rapid darting movements almost exactly similar to those another snake might make with its head, when striking at an enemy. And the pipe snake, an innocuous form which also has a red tail, behaves in almost precisely the same way. This is often cited as an example of mimetic behaviour, the harmless snake imitating the poisonous one. But it seems more reasonable to believe that in both instances, and in several similar cases where the tail is agitated and attracts attention, as in ring-neck snakes and in the Rubber boa (Plate 7), the behaviour has developed from a reaction originally associated with attracting prey or with diverting the predator's attention from the more vulnerable parts of the snake.

Sound warnings

Visual warnings and intimidatory behaviour are almost always accompanied by an audible warning, usually a hiss. No snakes have a true voice, but the volume of sound that can be produced by expelling air violently from the large lung is often surprisingly loud and startling and in a few instances, for example in some of the American gopher snakes, there is a membrane in the glottis that is set vibrating as the air rushes past it, to produce a staccato effect.

Audible warnings are also produced in other ways, but only by a few species. Rattlesnakes, of course, have their own peculiar device at the end of the tail (see Chap. 12 and Plate 16), but a number of other pit vipers, like the Bushmaster and the American copperhead, and some species belonging to other families, e.g. the Gopher snake and Sunbeam snake, vibrate the tips of their tails very rapidly to beat an audible tattoo on the ground, or to rustle the vegetation in which they are lying.

A form of stridulation is also practised by some of the Old World snakes, including the carpet vipers (Plate 15), the cerastes vipers, and the egg-eating snakes (Plate 8). The mechanism for this consists of a few rows of downward tilting flank scales which are equipped with large and serrated keels that make a grating sound when they are rubbed together. To produce the sound the body is drawn together in a series of side-to-side loops so tight that they are in contact and the animal forms a flat disc. Then a succession of new waves is formed near the head, and these travel towards the tail, displacing and replacing the older loops in their passage. As a result adjacent loops are continually moving past each other in opposite directions and their flank scales grate over each other as they pass.

The only other warning noise that has been recorded is made by three North American species – the Eastern and the Arizona coral snakes and the Western hook-nosed snake, all of which draw air in at the vent and expel it to produce a succession of popping sounds.

Feigning

When concealment, intimidation and warnings have all failed to divert or deter an enemy most snakes make a real or simulated attack, but a few first indulge in some form of passive resistance, adopting motionless attitudes that are not part of their concealing behaviour. Several of the smaller boas and pythons, kraits, king snakes and a few others roll themselves up into a tight ball with the head concealed in the middle, and others, like the Fishing snake, become absolutely rigid in an extended position and will not bend even when picked up and handled. The significance of these rigid postures is uncertain, but they seem to have something in common with increasing camouflage or with 'shamming dead', a phenomenon that can have a protective value only when the attacker's motive is fear or anger but not hunger.

Several of the arboreal dipsadine snakes (Chap. 10) fall limply to the ground when alarmed, and remain there completely inert; and the Ringhals, though equipped with another and highly effective means of defence (see below), will also roll over on its back as if dead. The most spectacular performance, however, is given by the American hognose snakes (Plate 10). Though they look superficially like vipers, these small snakes are not venomous but when alarmed they give a convincing display of apparently highly aggressive intentions, blowing themselves up, hissing violently and feinting with widely opened mouth. These threats, however, are not followed up by the expected attack; instead the snake rolls over onto its back, wriggles convulsively and then lies still with its mouth open and tongue lolling; if the 'dead' snake is turned over, it promptly rolls back again! The wide distribution of death-feigning suggests that it is successful in deterring predators.

48

Obnoxious secretions

Another peculiar response to interference is shown by the West Indian wood snakes. When molested these small boas coil up into a ball and at the same time produce an offensive-smelling anal secretion; immediately after this their eyes turn ruby-red with blood and a thin trickle of blood, from veins on the palate, dribbles slowly from the mouth. The foul-smelling anal discharge undoubtedly acts as a deterrent and it may be that the flow of blood has a similar effect. Many snakes are like the wood snakes in producing an anal secretion from a pair of sac-like glands in the base of the tail. In some instances this secretion may be used for laying a scent trail at the mating season but in most cases it appears to have no sexual significance and is discharged only when the snake is molested.

Counter-attack

Even when the last line of defence has been reached, the counter-attack in its initial stages may be more simulated than real; frequent lunges are made with apparent ferocity, but they fall short of the objective and sometimes the mouth is not even opened. It is also not unusual at this stage for the snake to uncoil itself stealthily to be ready for a speedy withdrawal and flight if the enemy recoils. But when an all-out attack finally develops, it follows the pattern usually employed in securing prey, though with increased ferocity; species that would normally bite and then release their victim, or merely hold it, bite repeatedly or worry their molester.

The venomous snakes, of course, have the weapons that are likely to be the most effective, but the larger constricting snakes enjoy one considerable advantage over them; an enemy once securely enmeshed in their coils is powerless to do them much harm, whereas a venomous snake may be severely mauled or killed before its venom has had time to take effect. A few cobras, e.g. the Ringhals and Black-necked cobra in Africa and some populations of the Indian cobra, have, however, developed a method of defensive attack without coming to close quarters; they 'spit' venom from a distance and although the poison is innocuous enough on the unbroken skin, if it enters an enemy's eyes it causes intense pain almost instantaneously and does considerable damage to the conjunctiva and cornea. The action is colloquially referred to as spitting, but this is not strictly correct. With its mouth half open the snake forcibly ejects venom through its fangs by muscular pressure on the venom glands, and, because the openings of the canals in the spitters are directed forward rather than downward, the poison issues as twin horizontal jets; the distance to which it is projected, up to about 2·5 metres, may be increased by a simultaneous blast of air from the glottis as the snake hisses.

7 Reproduction, growth and development

Reproduction

As previously mentioned (p. 32) the reproductive cycle may extend over two years in latitudes where the summer is short, but elsewhere breeding is normally an annual event. The usual pattern in the temperate zones is for the sex cells to complete their development during the winter months and for mating to occur in spring as soon as hibernation ends. There are, however, exceptions to this general rule and in a few species mating normally takes place in the summer, whilst even amongst the spring breeders there may be a recrudescence of mating activity in the autumn, as with many species of birds.

Finding a mate

Although it is not uncommon for a number of snakes to use the same 'den' for hibernation, they are for the most part solitary in their ways and finding a partner at the onset of the mating season may not be simple, the more so since their distant vision lacks clarity and they have neither voice nor acute hearing. So far as is known they all rely on scent to locate each other and for sex recognition; the male is almost always the active partner, but the female lays a scent trail. The secretion of the anal glands, as mentioned in the previous chapter, may have an offensive smell, at least to the human nose, when it is discharged in bulk, but in greater dilution it is apparently attractive to the males of some species. In other instances, however, it is not, and males have been observed to follow the path of a sexually mature female with a complete disregard of artificially laid cross trails of anal secretion.

Courtship

The pattern of courtship, which always precedes mating, varies greatly. Usually, as for example with the Grass snake, the female remains almost completely passive and the male approaches her, with his tongue flickering, until the underside of his chin, on which there are many very small sensory tubercles, rests on the hind part of her back. Then, with the tongue still constantly in play, he rubs his chin from side to side across her back. If, during this phase, the tubercles do not receive the appropriate stimulus, if, for instance, they have been covered

50

experimentally with adhesive tape or the female is of the wrong species, court-ship is discontinued. But if they are correctly stimulated the male gradually works his way forward, nodding his head and continuing to rub his chin across his partner's back, until he reaches the nape of her neck when he throws a loop of the hind part of his body across her back and their tails intertwine. In many of the boas and pythons the next phase of the courtship consists of the male using his claw-like vestigial hind limbs to scratch or stroke his mate's sides, but in 'limbless' snakes the male's body is thrown into a rapid series of rippling waves which run forwards from tail to head. If the female is not receptive these actions evoke no response and the partnership dissolves; but if she is physio-logically ready for reproduction she responds by opening her cloaca and coitus follows.

Combat dances

Ritualistic combat dances have been observed in a number of snakes including the Adder and other true vipers, pit vipers, mambas and other elapids, as well as colubrids. In the wild the dances take place between adult males of the same species and appear to be closely associated with mating behaviour, although the presence of a female does not seem to be essential to initiate the combat. While the dances may not always be the outcome of sexual rivalry other explana-tions such as social dominance or territorial behaviour are unlikely.

The most elaborate posture during the ritualistic struggle is that assumed by the Aesculapian snake of southern Europe. When a pair of rival males of this species meet, a series of headlong rushes begins and their bodies become inter-twined. Although locked together they rear up, their heads and necks nearly vertical and the foreparts of their bodies forming a lyre-shaped figure. In this position they make lunges at each other and the whole sequence may be repeated several times.

Other colubrids in which combat dances have been observed (the Dhaman and American Gopher snake) barely raise their heads from the ground. Like the Aesculapian snake, but not to the same degree, contesting male mambas, vipers and pit vipers rear up off the ground and, locked together, rise higher and higher, pressing against each other until one is forced to give way and retreat from the arena. The kerykeion, the ancient insignia of Hermes, and the symbol of the medical profession may be based on the combat dance of male Aescula-pian snakes.

Fig. 17. The combat dance of male Sand vipers *(Vipera ammodytes)* with tails entwined and foreparts raised. (Based on a photograph by Thomas 1960.)

Egg-laying and birth

Although there are a few instances where there seems to be a considerable time-lag before the eggs are fertilized after mating, in most cases this occurs at once. The time that elapses before the eggs are laid varies. The Grass snake (fig. 18), for instance, normally pairs in Britain during April or early May, but the eggs are not deposited until two to three months later, by which time embryonic development is well advanced. The interval between the two events varies from species to species and reaches its maximum in viviparous forms which, like the Smooth snake (fig. 19) and the Adder, retain their eggs until they are on the point of hatching. Snakes' eggs, whether or not they are retained like this, contain all the nutritive material required for the full development of the young, except water and oxygen which reach the foetus by diffusion through the egg-shell.

In oviparous species, where there is a relatively long incubation period outside the mother's body, the eggs are provided with a tough, protective, parchment-like shell, but in viparous forms where there is not the same need for protection the shell is no more than a thin transparent membrane.

Water and oxygen are, of course, freely available from the outside world when the eggs are laid, but as there is no free circulation of atmospheric oxygen inside the oviducts, foetal requirements in viviparous species have to be supplied from the maternal bloodstream by way of the capillary blood vessels in their epithelial lining. This has led in a few instances (e.g. some garter snakes, the Australian copperhead, some sea snakes and the Adder) to the development of a very simple type of placenta, a structure which brings the blood vessels of mother and foetus

52

Fig. 18. The Grass snake *(Natrix natrix)*; the commoner of the two harmless British snakes. Each scale of the body has a central ridge (keel) and the upper surface of the head has enlarged plates; the pupil is circular, unlike the venomous British Adder.
Photo: Geoffrey Kinns

very close together. In mammals, where the eggs are almost always minute and contain very little nutritive material, the placenta provides the channel through which all the foodstuffs for the developing young are supplied, but in snakes, where it is a more primitive structure, it probably transmits little more than oxygen and water.

Incubation. Most oviparous snakes deposit their eggs in shallow holes and cover them with a thin layer of soil that not only conceals them but stabilizes the temperature, protecting them from the too great heat of the sun's direct rays and from the low temperatures of the night. Temperature control, involving careful selection of the nesting site, is vitally important because the rate of development of the eggs is directly related to their temperature. Numerous individuals may select the same site in which to lay their eggs and aggregations of hundreds of eggs have been reported. The incubation period varies with the weather and climate, and because at high altitudes and latitude air and soil

53

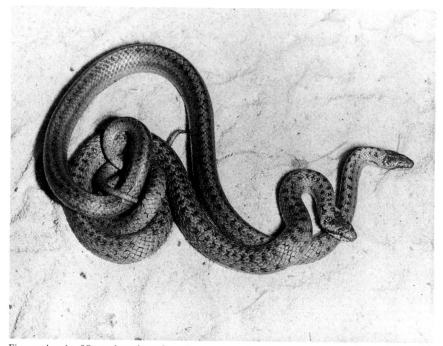

Fig. 19. A pair of Smooth snakes *(Coronella austriaca)*; the rarer of the two harmless British snakes. Its numbers have seriously declined and it is now a protected species in Britain. Photo: Geoffrey Kinns

temperatures may be too low to allow successful hatching of the eggs, few oviparous snakes range far into these marginal climatic areas. In viviparous forms, however, the mother is at all times actively endeavouring to maintain her own body temperature within the optimum range of about 21–37°C (see Chap. 4) so that the eggs are provided with far more favourable temperature conditions for rapid development; hence the snakes that have penetrated farthest towards the polar regions or the glaciated zones of the high mountain ranges are all viviparous.

A few egg-laying forms have nevertheless developed habits that secure for their eggs higher and more uniform temperatures than are to be found where conditions are determined by the climate alone. The Grass snake, for instance, whenever possible nests in sites where decaying organic matter maintains a steady temperature that is scarcely affected by the vagaries of the weather. Hayricks, dung piles, compost heaps and similar situations, mostly resulting from man's activities, are commonly used, and eggs laid in such places hatch several weeks before those laid where there is no supplementary heat. It is consequently not surprising that this species *(Natrix natrix)*, which carries its eggs like a viviparous snake for two months and then provides them with an extraneous source of

54

warmth, has been almost as successful as the completely viviparous Adder in its penetration of the subarctic regions; it extends to 67°N in Sweden.

Several other snakes, including the Aesculapian snake in Europe, the Aurora snake in Africa and several cobras, kraits, pit vipers and pythons, also make use of decomposing organic matter for incubating their eggs. In most instances they rely on naturally occurring or man-made piles of vegetation, but a few, like the Hamadryad, construct their own mounds; dead leaves and loose vegetation are scraped together by loops of the body and the eggs are laid at the bottom of the pile. The female Hamadryad also coils up over the eggs and remains there, almost continuously, until they hatch; and it has been claimed that Indian pythons, which have similar 'brooding' habits, can raise and maintain their body temperature to assist incubation; temperatures higher than that of the surrounding air by as much as 7°C have been recorded. The 'brooding' habit and coiled body give a measure of temperature control as well as protection because the mother can cover or uncover her eggs at will as the weather varies and so ensure a more uniform, and probably higher, temperature; at the same time coiling reduces the exposed surfaces.

The limitations of viviparity

Although viviparity has clear advantages for many terrestrial and especially arboreal species and is essential for a completely aquatic life, it nevertheless has its disadvantages. The pregnant female, with her activity and agility reduced by her burden of young, is more likely to fall a victim to enemies as well as being less able to secure her own food. This handicap is sometimes mitigated by reducing the size of the litter. Of the three British snakes, for example, the average clutch-size of the Grass snake is between 30 and 40 whereas the litters of the other two, viviparous, species range from 4 to 15 in the case of the Smooth snake and from 6 to 20 in the Adder. However, in spite of the fact that some of the sea snakes have litters of no more than one or two, a few other viviparous forms may be at least as prolific as many oviparous species. The Puff adder, for instance, often has litters of between 60 and 80, some rattlesnakes up to 60 and the Common garter snake as many as 78. However it is likely that a much smaller complement is more typical of the species because few species of snakes have more than 50 eggs per clutch or young per litter.

Early development

Hatching

The eggs contain at least sufficient yolk to enable the young to reach a size and stage of development at which they can fend for themselves immediately they leave the egg, and sometimes there is a safety margin large enough to enable them to go into hibernation almost at once. A day or two before the eggs hatch –

Fig. 20. Indian Cobra *(Naja naja)* emerging from its egg.
Photo: Michael Lyster: copyright Zoological Society of London

when foetal development is nearly complete – the yolk sac is drawn into the body cavity and its surplus material absorbed into the intestine, thus leaving a slit-like umbilical scar just in front of the vent. The young of oviparous species have a special tooth with which they cut their way out of the eggshell. The tooth erupts from the gum at the tip of the premaxilla on the mid line. In structure it is a normal dentine-covered tooth but it projects beyond the snout and has a razor-like cutting edge. When the young snake has slashed a sufficiently large hole in the shell the head emerges and after a rest, perhaps lasting a whole day, the young one crawls out (fig. 20). The egg-tooth, its function fulfilled, is then sloughed.

In viviparous forms, where the eggs hatch as they are being laid, or immediately afterwards, the eggshell is so fragile that egg-teeth are not only unnecessary but might be a danger to the mother as the young ones struggle to escape; nevertheless they are still present, but are usually bent downwards or downwards and backwards so that their sharp tips do not project and sometimes they are vestigial and may even be shed before the egg-membrane is ruptured.

Newly born or hatchlings of some species of snake seem almost incredibly large in relation to the eggs in which they have developed. Young Grass snakes emerging from eggs barely 3 cm long are 15–17 cm long and Adders, whose unlaid

56

eggs are comparable in size, give birth to young ones between 12 and 17 cm long. Generally the smaller the brood or litter the larger the newly born or hatchling. While in some viviparous species the newly born are half the normal length of the adult female the Fer-de-lance is exceptional in giving birth to small and numerous young. No snakes are able to feed their young and few show the slightest sign of parental care of any kind.

Growth

There are very few reliable observations on the rate of growth of snakes in the wild state, and records based on captive specimens are conflicting. Depending as it does on variable factors such as temperature and feeding conditions, the rate must vary greatly, and diminish with age, though perhaps never ceasing completely. Statistical evidence based on wild populations of the Adder in northern Europe suggests that males increase in length by nearly 50 per cent in their first year but that each subsequent year's increase is only about four-fifths of what it was in the year before. Ideally, therefore, with an average length of 160 mm at birth, male adders should average about 240, 304, 356 and 397 mm in length at one to four years of age and the observed averages were 240, 310, 360 and 400 mm. Furthermore this pattern of growth would result in a maximum average length (asymptotic limit) of about 565 mm, which would be nearly reached in fifteen years when the annual increase would have fallen to less than 3·5 mm; in Britain the average of the five largest recorded males is 569 mm.

In females, however, when sexual maturity is reached and breeding commences large amounts of nutritive material have to be diverted to egg production and a check in the rate of growth is to be expected. As if to compensate for this the growth rate in early life is appreciably higher, nearly 70 per cent in the first year. This would give an asymptotic limit of about 660 mm if there were no breeding check; but the average length of the five largest recorded British specimens is significantly less than this – 605 mm.

Puberty

The age of puberty varies with the size of the species and is, naturally, also affected by the environmental conditions. In Britain all three of the native species become sexually mature in about their fourth year when they are two-thirds grown and the first litters or egg clutches are produced in the fourth or fifth year. In North America, too, in comparable latitudes several of the rattle-snakes, e.g. Prairie rattlesnake, Great Basin rattlesnake and North Pacific rattle-snake, mature at about the same age. But the same three species have a wide geographical distribution and range southwards into states where the climate is nearly subtropical and there puberty is reached in the third year. There is, at present, insufficient information available for safe generalization, but in the tropics where sexual activity usually proceeds throughout the year some species attain sexual maturity in under two years and one species, *Pareas carinatus* of the Indo-Chinese region, Malaysia and Indonesia, has been reported to breed at eleven months.

Classification of snakes followed in this book

infraorder	family*	subfamily
SCOLECOPHIDIA	Leptotyphlopidae	
	Typhlopidae	
	Anomalepididae	
HENOPHIDIA	Aniliidae	
	Uropeltidae	
	Xenopeltidae	
	Boidae	Boinae
		Erycinae
		Tropidophiinae
		Calabariinae
		Pythoninae
		Loxoceminae
		Bolyeriinae
	Acrochordidae	
CAENOPHIDIA	Colubridae	Xenodermatinae
		Pareinae
		Dipsadinae
		Dasypeltinae
		Homalopsinae
		Colubrinae
		Natricinae
		Aparallactinae
	Elapidae	Elapinae
		Hydrophiinae
		Laticaudinae
	Viperidae	Azemiopinae
		Viperinae
		Crotalinae

* Table 4, p. 95, summarizes some of the characteristics of the eleven families.

8 *Primitive and burrowing snakes*

In Chapter 2 attention was drawn to the occurrence in a minority of snakes of features that are essentially lizard-like, and Table 3 shows the position clearly. Twenty-seven 'characters' are listed which differentiate most species of snakes from most lizards and in twenty of these the snakes show no variability. In the remaining seven, however, snakes are variable, and in every single instance the condition that is rare or unusual for them is normal for lizards. Since there can be no question that snakes have evolved from lizard-like ancestors, and not vice versa, it seems certain that the unusual condition (e.g. possession of hind limbs, a jugal bone, an immovable supratemporal, two lungs, or the absence of a tracheal lung, etc.) is, with one exception, due to the retention of an ancestral (i.e. 'primitive') condition that has been lost or changed in most species.

The exception concerns the gastrosteges which are an ophidian development and their absence in some groups of snakes may be primitive and, in others, secondary; the method of locomotion that depends upon gastrosteges may never have been acquired or it may have been abandoned with consequent loss of the structures. Thus, some of the sea snakes have no gastrosteges, but others have them and it is clear that in this group their absence is a secondary loss; they are not required for swimming. But in some other groups of burrowing snakes, where they are also lacking, their absence may be primitive. The primitive characters do not appear at random in all groups of snakes but are restricted to a few clearly recognizable families each of which has one or more of them. These families are dealt with in this chapter.

Thread snakes – Family LEPTOTYPHLOPIDAE

The members of this group, and the next two families to be mentioned, are the most highly specialized for subterranean life, and in one very important respect they have evolved in a direction diametrically opposed to all other snakes – the size of the mouth has been drastically reduced, and is only about half as long as the head. The jawbones are extremely short but, to compensate for this the quadrate bone, which provides the hinge for the lower jaw, is

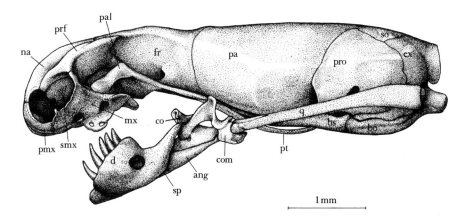

Fig. 21. Skull of a thread snake *(Leptotyphlops macrolepis)*. Key to abbreviations p. 7.

lengthened to form a rod that runs forwards almost horizontally from the hind end of the cranium (fig. 21).

The thread snakes usually retain a comparatively well-developed pelvic girdle and sometimes vestigial hind limbs (which may project as horny claws) whilst, except for the lower jaws, the skull lacks flexibility; the upper jawbones are rigidly attached to each other and to the bones of the snout; coronoid bones are present, and there are no gastrosteges. These are probably primitive features, but in other respects the snakes are degenerate or specialized. Supratemporal bones seem to be absent and all the bones of the upper jaw and palate have lost their teeth; there is only one lung and one oviduct (the right), whilst the eye is small, simple but fully differentiated and lacks a brille.

There are about fifty species (two genera – *Leptotyphlops* and *Rhinoleptus*) which occur in the more arid, but not truly desert, areas of Africa, southwestern Asia and the New World from the southern United States to Argentina. None is more than 38 cm long and all are worm-like and very slender, fifty to a hundred times as long as they are broad. The head is bluntly rounded or sometimes slightly hooked in profile; the scales of the body are thick, highly polished, and very strongly overlapping; and the tail is short, usually less than a tenth of the total length, and blunt (Plate 1).

61

The rigid, toothless upper jaws and the stoutly built lower jaws with few though relatively large and stout teeth (fig. 21) are not compatible with the requirements for swallowing bulky prey. Their food consists of termites, ants and other soft-bodied arthropods which are seized at the hind end of the soft abdomen; the jaws are then worked rapidly forwards, the contents of the abdomen being sucked out, until the chitinous head is reached, when the snake writhes energetically and brushes the arthropod from its mouth.

'Blind' snakes – Family TYPHLOPIDAE

The members of this family (about 180 species) are referred to as 'blind' snakes. However, this may be misleading, for although their eyes are very small they are quite well developed. They bear a strong superficial resemblance to the thread snakes with their reduced eyes, small mouths, thick, polished and strongly overlapping scales, short, blunt tails and worm-like build; and, internally, the two groups are also similar in having a pelvis and a single (right) oviduct whilst the left lung and supratemporal bones are vestigial or absent. There are, however, notable differences. Although the premaxilla is toothless, like the palate, and rigidly attached to the snout, the maxillae are toothed (fig. 22), and are only loosely articulated to the skull so that they are capable of a certain amount of independent movement; and the lower jaw is rigid and toothless. Furthermore, unlike the thread snakes, they have a tracheal lung and no enlarged scale in front of the anus. The genera of 'blind' snakes differ radically in the male copulatory organ. In *Typhlops* it is an eversible tube typical of the Squamata, but in *Ramphotyphlops* it is a solid protrusible structure.

Distributed in the warmer temperate and tropical countries the blind snakes are essentially subterranean creatures, though some are only shallow burrowers, and many species have a hooked snout with a sharp, horizontal cutting edge on the very large shield that covers its tip and takes the impact when they are tunnelling. Their food consists of small invertebrates, especially ants.

Family ANOMALEPIDIDAE

Some twenty Central and South American species currently referred to four genera, *Liotyphlops*, *Helminthophis*, *Typhlophis* and *Anomalepis*, resemble the thread snakes and 'blind' snakes in habits, appearance and in many anatomical features but differ from them in lacking any vestiges of a pelvis, and in some other important features of the skeleton. Although the maxillae are toothed and movable, the frontal bones are shorter and the prefrontal bones, with which the maxillae articulate, extend backwards over the orbits; this latter condition is found in no other group of snakes. They further differ from the previous two families in having a long, slender lower jaw which is hinged and which rarely bears more than one small tooth. Only *Helminthophis* lacks a left oviduct.

62

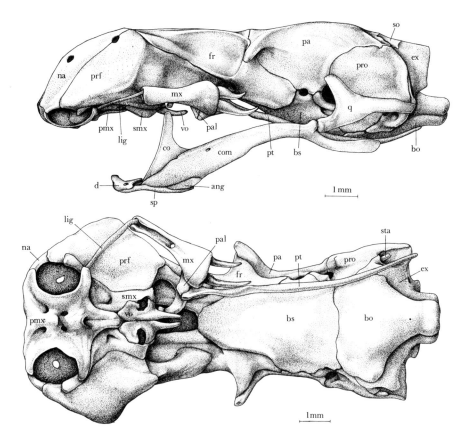

Fig. 22. Skull of a 'blind' snake *(Typhlops punctatus)*. Above. Lateral view. Below. Ventral view with lower jaws and right upper jaw removed. Three empty tooth sockets in maxilla not visible in figure. Key to abbreviations p. 7.

Pipe snakes and Anilius – Family ANILIIDAE

This family consists of a single species *(Anilius scytale)* from northern South America, and about nine pipe snakes (genera *Anomochilus* and *Cylindrophis*) from southeastern Asia, from Burma and Vietnam southwards to Borneo and the islands of Indonesia with one species in Sri Lanka. These snakes have a pelvis with vestigial hind limbs and a primitive type of skull (fig. 23) in which almost the only provision for the swallowing of bulky prey is the elastic ligamentous union of the two rami of the lower jaw. The mouth is not enlarged and the

63

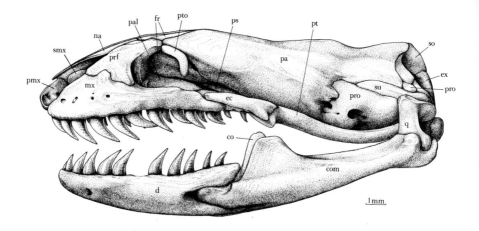

Fig. 23. Skull of the Malaysian pipe snake *(Cylındrophis rufus)*. Key to abbreviations p. 7.

hinges of the lower jaw are approximately level with the hind end of the brain-case, the quadrate bone being very short and vertical and forming a broad attachment with the large paroccipital process. The bones of the upper jaw and snout are not movable on each other or on the cranium, and each ramus of the lower jaw, too, is rigid, with a small coronoid bone at the junction of the dentary and angular. In consequence there is little flexibility or distensibility of the mouth and this restricts the diet; the pipe snakes, which, when not prowling in search of food, spend most of their lives burrowing in the soft earth of cultivated land, feed principally on slender animals, such as other snakes, and *Anilius* eats caecilians (limbless, worm-like amphibians) and amphisbaenians.

All the species resemble the more advanced, typical, snakes in the left lung being absent or reduced to about 10 per cent of the right lung, and in possessing gastrosteges, but there are important differences between the forms of the New World and those of Asia, differences that suggest they ought, perhaps, to be placed in different subfamilies. Thus, in the pipe snakes the premaxillary bone has lost its teeth and the eye is relatively well developed with its own, circular, protective scale – the brille. In *Anilius*, however, premaxillary teeth are retained (a primitive feature), but the eye, though still visible, is somewhat degenerate and lies beneath a relatively large, transparent polygonal scale.

64

Shield-tails – Family Uropeltidae

Whereas the previous family shows a trend away from the primitive towards the more 'advanced' snakes that are, for the most part, active, surface-dwelling or climbing creatures, the shield-tails (Plate 1) are specialized for a subterranean existence. They retain a primitive inflexible (akinetic) skull resembling that of the Aniliidae, with a short vertical quadrate and rigid jaws (the lower retaining the coronoid), but there is loss of the pelvis and the hind limbs; orbital bones are absent, the supratemporal is vestigial and teeth are absent not only from the premaxilla but also, except in two genara, from the whole of the palatal region. As in other specialized burrowing families there is, in most species, no brille, the small degenerate eye being covered by a large polygonal shield. Gastrosteges are very much reduced. The left lung is usually present although very small.

The family is, however, unique in three other features affecting the tip of the tail and the mobility of the head. The end of the tail either has an enlarged ridged scale with two points or, more frequently, its upper surface has a subcircular area covered with thickened spiny scales or a single much enlarged spiny plate (Plate 1). The tail tip is supported internally by a bony plate that abuts on the spine.

The neck modifications are associated with the exceptional features of the first two vertebrae. The disappearance of the inter-centrum of the atlas and the odontoid process of the axis allows the extraordinarily long backwardly projecting occipital condyle to form a ball and socket joint with the axis. Such peculiar morphology does not occur in any other group of snakes, but clearly it allows the snake to bend its head to an unusual angle, and even preserved specimens often have a wry neck. .

The functional significance of this unique neck modification seems to be associated with the method employed by uropeltids to tunnel and avoid obstructions. As the narrow pointed snout forces its way through the soil, the neck makes a series of sharp, sinuous movements which sufficiently increase the width of the burrow to allow the stouter body to be drawn up behind. Similarly the neck mobility allows the snake to circumnavigate readily any stone or other obstruction in its path.

A shield-tail when alarmed has a tendency to tuck its head in among the body coils and extrude and agitate its tail. As the spines on the tail tip collect a coating of soil particles and mud the tail waving may serve to protect the head of the snake from its enemies.

The shield-tails, of which there are about forty species, are found in the mountains and foothills of peninsular India and throughout Sri Lanka. Varying in adult size from about 20 to 75 cm they form deep tunnels in soft earth and subsist mainly

65

on earthworms. Some are brilliantly coloured, with red, orange or yellow markings, but others are uniformly black and highly iridescent.

Sunbeam snakes – Family XENOPELTIDAE

The Sunbeam snake (Plate 2), a common and very inoffensive snake of the Indo-Malaysian region, ranging from Burma and southern China to the Indonesian islands, is unique in its combination of primitive and advanced features. It has a pair of lungs and also a primitive, inflexible type of skull like that of *Anilius* with a short, vertical quadrate, immovable supratemporal, suturally united upper jaw elements, premaxillary teeth and no postfrontal bone. Its lower jaw, however, is very flexible indeed, the dentary being only loosely linked with the angular. The mouth is, therefore, somewhat more flexible than that of the preceding family and the diet is less restricted; in addition to snakes, frogs and small mammals are eaten.

In its general appearance the Sunbeam snake bears a resemblance to typical colubrids, and like them has no pelvic girdle but possesses gastrosteges and a brille; however, its true affinities may lie with the primitive boid, *Loxocemus*.

The Sunbeam snake is a semi-burrowing, crepuscular creature reaching a length of just over a metre. It is black to chocolate brown in colour with the scales of the lower flanks and belly edged with white; its name derives from the beautiful iridescence of its highly polished scales.

9 *Boas, pythons and wart snakes*

The families discussed in the previous chapter have either lost or, more probably, have never acquired the large mouth and flexible skull necessary for swallowing bulky prey. In the remaining families, however, the elements of the skull that compose the snout, jaws and palate are capable of a certain amount of independent movement (see Chap. 2), which results in a flexible and distensible mouth; and the mouth itself is proportionally larger, and the hinder part of the palate and the lower jaw having been lengthened so that the angles of the gape are situated behind the occipital region of the cranium.

This backward extension of the mouth necessitates a backward migration of the lower end of the quadrate on which the jaw hinges and this adjustment is brought about either by elongation of the bone itself, so that it projects obliquely backwards from the skull, or by a similar elongation of the supratemporal bone or by a combination of the two (fig. 1 D). In many forms increased flexibility in this region is achieved by the development of a movable joint between the quadrate and the supratemporal; the latter may also be movably articulated at its point of attachment to the skull.

Boas and pythons – Family BOIDAE

In the boas and their relatives the supratemporal bones are elongated (fig. 24) as are the quadrates, though to a lesser extent; and both are freely movable so that when they are swung sideways to their full extent the distance between the hinges of the lower jaw is greatly increased.

Primitive features found in nearly all of them are a comparatively rigid lower jaw, with a coronoid element, a pelvis with vestigial hind limbs (fig. 4), and a long row of palatal teeth; most have a functional left lung that may be three-quarters the size of the right and some also have postfrontal bones and premaxillary teeth. Since none is fully aquatic or completely subterranean they all have gastrosteges and well-developed eyes with a brillar scale-covering, and most of them are heavily built.

The boids are an ancient group (fossils of Cretaceous age are known) and this long history is reflected in so much diversity amongst the forms that have sur-

67

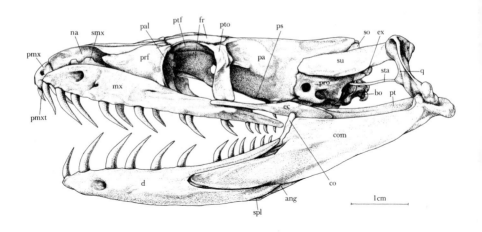

Fig. 24. Skull of the African rock python *(Python sebae)*. Key to abbreviations p. 7.

vived to the present day that at least seven subfamilies can be recognized. The most primitive subfamily is perhaps the Central American LOXOCEMINAE (one genus). It possesses the primitive features of a postfrontal bone (often referred to as a supraorbital) and premaxillary teeth, as well as jaw muscles that are more primitive than in any other member of the family. The Sunbeam snake *(Xenopeltis)*, discussed in the previous chapter, seems to be closely related to the Loxoceminae and may actually belong to this group.

The subfamily PYTHONINAE consists of about twenty species of large pythons occurring in Africa, and the Oriental, Indonesian, Papuan and Australian regions. As in *Loxocemus* there is a postfrontal bone (fig. 24) and all except *Aspidites* also have the primitive feature of teeth on the premaxillary bone.

The best known forms are the true pythons (genus *Python*, (Plate 4)) and these include the two largest snakes of the Old World, the reticulated python, which ranges from southern Burma to Flores and reaches a length of 10 metres and the African rock python (Plate 3) which has been recorded up to 9·75 metres.

Most of the pythons are active marauders with a fairly wide tolerance of environmental conditions; they are frequently to be found in or near water but many of them have more or less prehensile tails and are equally at home in trees and bushes. Large Reticulated pythons can be a danger to humans and may in

68

exceptional circumstances attack them (see Chap. 5). Their food consists almost entirely of warm-blooded animals and they are reported to have a special type of sense organ to assist them in locating their prey.

The Australian rock snakes *(Aspidites)* are the only large pythons that lack deeply concave pits within the margins of the scales bordering the upper lips. The keratinous lining of these concavities is much thinner than that of the other, more exposed, scales of the head and body and, like the diaphragm in the facial pit of crotaline vipers, it is very sensitive to infra-red radiation (fig. 25). It not only registers the proximity of objects warmer than their surroundings but when, as is often the case, the apertures of the pits are narrow and slit-like a directional sense is added; only rays coming from an appropriate angle are able to enter squarely into any one of the pits which face radially outwards round the periphery of a rough semicircle.

The Calabar ground python (Plate 5) may be placed in a subfamily of its own, the CALABARIINAE. It is not more than about a metre long, and is mainly subter-ranean in habits; it spends most of its life burrowing in search of small rodents and shrews and is unique in the family in lacking any teeth on the bones of the palate. It is usually referred to as a python since it has a postfrontal but it has a more compact skull than any other member of the family. It lacks pits and it has affinities with both boas and pythons.

The large boas (subfamily BOINAE) differ from the Pythoninae in the absence of postfrontal bones and of premaxillary teeth and in being viviparous. They further differ in the position of the labial pits which, where present (three genera), occur between and not on the scales. However, because the two groups are so very similar in other respects, and especially in their adaptations to similar environmental conditions, these may seem to be very trivial differences; but it is significant that the two groups are almost completely mutually exclusive in their geographical distribution. Thus there are no pythons in the Americas or in Malagasy, only boas, of which there are seven genera ($\pm$ 19 species) in the former region and two genera (3 species) in the latter; and again, from southeastern Asia and Australia there are only pythons whilst farther east, in Melanesia and Polynesia, there are dwarf boas *(Candoia,* 3 species) but no pythons. In the few areas where the two groups coexist they tend to occupy different habitats. In Africa and the Indian subcontinent the pythons are more closely associated with grassland and forest whereas the only boas are the small sand boas *(Eryx* (Plate 4), 10 species) which as their name indicates are confined to the more arid regions. In the New Guinea region the pythons are sympatric with *Candoia,* a small streamside inhabitant.

The true *Boa constrictor,* of which there are several geographical races ranging from Mexico (Plate 3) and the Lesser Antilles to Argentina, is an unspecialized terrestrial or subarboreal species with a slightly prehensile tail and a wide

69

Fig. 25. Royal python *Python regius* showing clearly the heat sensitive pits on the upper lip. Photo: British Museum (Natural History): courtesy Zoological Society of London

tolerance of differing climatic conditions; it is found in all types of country from arid, near-deserts to humid tropical forests. Despite popular belief it is not an exceptionally large snake, the maximum length recorded being 5·6 metres; nor is it capable of eating the gargantuan meals recorded in some travellers' tales. The prey consists mainly of birds and mammals, but curiously enough the Boa constrictor has no obvious temperature sensing pits around the mouth (Plate 3), although these organs are present between the labial scales in the tropical American genera *Epicrates* and *Corallus* and the Malagasy *Sanzinia*. These snakes are distinctly, though not exclusively, arboreal in habits and are also largely nocturnal, so that possibly the labial pits are concerned with the detection of roosting birds and bats.

No other boas have labial pits, though some of them have slightly prehensile tails. The best known of these occasional climbers is the Anaconda, which is aquatic-arboreal, being found in or near sluggish fresh water or amongst trees and bushes on the banks of pools and streams. Although it spends much of its life in water, fish form but a small part of its diet and it preys mainly on the birds and mammals that come to the water to drink, with an occasional caiman or freshwater turtle. Ranging over the northern half of South America it shows a considerable amount of local geographical variation and the northernmost race, *Eunectes murinus gigas*, is the largest serpent still in existence. Specimens longer than 9 metres are rare but there is one credible record that suggests a maximum length of about 11·4 metres.

Although most of the boas are, as indicated, terrestrial-arboreal or aquatic-arboreal, a few have adopted a cryptozoic or semi-burrowing existence. These, the ERYCINAE, are all of small size, less than 1 metre in length, with stumpy conical tails and small conical heads that merge into the body without any narrower neck, and include the Rosy boa and Rubber boa (Plate 7) of North America and the sand boas (Plate 4) of the Old World. The first two of these are generally rather docile, their defence reaction consisting of rolling themselves up into a ball (Chap. 6). Some sand boas are, however, aggressive and their attack is not the usual lunge and bite, but a series of very rapid sidelong slashing bites which result in deep lacerations. Many of the sand boas have a horizontal ridge across the tip of the snout, like some of the 'blind' snakes, to assist in burrowing, and their nostrils may be narrow slits to exclude earth and sand from the respiratory tract.

Four genera of dwarf boas are contained in the TROPIDOPHIINAE, two of them (*Ungaliophis* and *Exiliboa*) only tentatively referred to the group. They occur in Central America, northern South America and the West Indies, and while they resemble other boids in most of their anatomical features, they differ in having a well-developed tracheal lung; female *Ungaliophis* is exceptional among boids in lacking vestiges of hind limbs. They further differ from most if not all pythons and the rest of the boas in having almost or completely lost their left lung. Only one of the species has arboreal tendencies, all the others are terrestrial or secretive. The best known members of the group are the wood snakes whose curious defence reactions were described in Chapter 6.

Amongst the most interesting snakes, from the standpoint of their origin, relationship and geographical distribution, are the BOLYERIINAE from Round Island, in the Indian Ocean near Mauritius. Two species, *Bolyeria multicarinata* and *Casarea dussumieri*, have been found on this tiny and inaccessible islet, and subfossil remains of a third, extinct, species have been found on Mauritius. Superficially they look like medium-sized boas but they differ from all other boids in the absence, in both sexes, of vestiges of hind limbs or a pelvis and from the pythons and large boas in a greater reduction in the size of the left lung. In these and some other respects too, they resemble the typical snakes (Colubridae) but they are unique among amniotes in having the upper jawbone (maxilla) divided into two at about the middle of its length, with the two halves loosely and flexibly connected to each other. Nevertheless the mouth is not greatly elongated (supratemporals and quadrates are shorter than in most boas) and the lower jaw has retained its rigidity, with the coronoid element persisting.

The Tropidophiinae and the Bolyeriinae have a greater number of higher snake features than any other member of the Boidae and their fragmented and widely separated distribution suggests that they may be relics of an early boa-like stock from which the Colubridae arose.

Wart snakes – Family ACROCHORDIDAE

The wart snakes, of which there are only two species, both in the Indo-Australian region, are highly specialized for aquatic life in rivers and coastal, mainly estuarine, waters. In many essential features, for example, a single lung, the absence of hind limbs and pelvis, a kinetic skull and a flexible lower jaw lacking the coronoid bone, they resemble the Colubridae, but they differ in several other respects. The supratemporals, though large and freely movable on the cranium, are relatively short whilst the elongated quadrates, instead of being articulated with them, are rigidly attached. The postorbital has a forward T-shaped extension. The single (right) lung extends back as far as the cloaca and the tracheal lung is also well developed and vascular.

Some of the specializations of the wart snakes are also found in other aquatic, but not closely related, forms. For example, there are no gastrosteges, eyes and nostrils are directed more upwards than sideways and the tail, though slightly prehensile, is somewhat flattened from side to side; and one of the species – the Asiatic file snake *Chersydrus granulatus* (Plate 5), which ranges from the coasts of India and Sri Lanka to northern Australia and the Solomon Islands – also has the skin of the belly raised into a ridge, like a low median fin, which increases lateral resistance and improves swimming efficiency.

Some of their other aquatic modifications, however, are unique. To exclude water from the respiratory tract when they are submerged, instead of the external nostrils being valvular, there is a backwardly directed flap in the roof of the mouth that closes the internal openings of the nasal passages; and the deep notch in the middle of the upper lip, through which the tips of the tongue are protruded when the tongue is in use as a sense organ, can be closed by a pad on the tip of the chin. Their skin and scales, too, are almost unique. The former is extraordinarily loose and baggy whilst the scales have the form of small, non-overlapping tubercular or wart-like granules (whence the name of the group) which make the skin attractive to the fancy-leather manufacturers; the tanned skin of the larger of the species, the Elephant-trunk snake, is sold as 'Karung'.

The wart snakes are obese, sluggish creatures, more active by night than by day, and are almost helpless on land. Their diet consists exclusively of fish (see Chap. 5) and both species are viviparous, the Elephant-trunk snake being very prolific, with litters of 25 to 32.

10 *Colubrid snakes*

Egg-eaters, slug-eaters, racers, whip snakes and their relatives – Family COLUBRIDAE

Of the three thousand or so kinds of snakes living in the world today more than two-thirds belong to the family COLUBRIDAE. This group, comprising the 'typical', mostly harmless, species (Plate 10), forms the dominant element of the snake faunas of all the continents except Australia, where the venomous Elapidae (Chap. 11) are in the majority.

Naturally, within such a large group there is a considerable range of diversity, adaptation and specialization, but none of them has any traces of a pelvis or hind limbs, all have the left lung much reduced or absent, gastrosteges are uniformly present, whilst the tail is rarely prehensile and never paddle-shaped; the skull is always highly kinetic with a flexible lower jaw that lacks the coronoid element and, in the majority, there is elongation of the quadrate bones and usually of the supratemporal too and the postfrontal is always absent; there are no perforated venom fangs at the front of the mouth but solid teeth are present on both jaws and on the palate, though not on the premaxilla.

Although no completely satisfactory scheme of subfamily divisions has yet been devised it is convenient to recognize a few small groups of aberrant or specialized forms that seem to represent evolutionary side-shoots from the main stock. For example, the XENODERMATINAE comprising four genera in southeastern Asia (*Xenodermus, Achalinus, Fimbrios* and *Stoliczkaia*) may represent a link between the wart snakes (discussed in the previous chapter) and the Colubridae. Although as terrestrial snakes they have gastrosteges and no aquatic respiratory modifications, they resemble the wart snakes in some features, notably in possessing a forward extension of the postorbital. The body scales of the Xenodermatinae show a gradation between the unique acrochordid condition of non-overlapping, widely separated granules and the typical colubrine condition.

Little is known of the biology of these snakes, which seem to be mainly nocturnal in their habits, and they possess some remarkable and unexplained modifications of their vertebrae. In *Xenodermus* the tips of the neural spines (fig. 7)

73

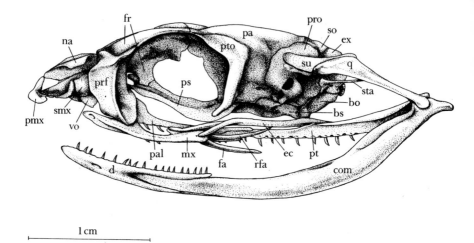

├─────────── 1 cm ───────────┤

Fig. 26. Skull of the Boomslang *(Dispholidus typus)*. Key to abbreviations p. 7.

are expanded in the horizontal plane to form flat, bony plates with a median groove; *Stoliczkaia* lacks these plates but the pre- and postzygapophyses (fig. 7) are both greatly enlarged to form wing-like lateral expansions and similar lateral wings are also present in *Xenodermus*.

Some groups of colubrids are modified in connection with a restricted diet. Snails, for example, are not a generally favoured food (their shells being too hard to be penetrated by a snake's teeth) though very small ones may sometimes be swallowed; and some snakes, like the African slug-eater (Plate 8), deal with larger ones by smashing their shells on the ground as some birds do. But one group of species in Asia (the PAREINAE) and another group in America (the DIPSADINAE) are almost exlusively mollusc eaters and have evolved a simple technique for extracting snails from their shells. The soft parts of a wandering snail are seized and a grip is maintained as it attempts to withdraw into its shell. Then the snake thrusts its lower jaw forwards into the opening of the shell, hooks its mandibular teeth into the soft tissues and retracts the jaw again, dragging the snail out.

74

To be successful this technique requires three things: a lower jaw that can be protracted and retracted a long way without any corresponding movements of the upper jaw and palate; strong, recurved teeth at the tip of the lower jaw; and a blunt snout that will not get drawn into the snail's shell as the victim contracts. Both the Dipsadinae and the Pareinae have a characteristic short, blunt and very deep snout and the bones of the upper jaw and palate are not connected to the quadrates which are very long and free to swing in a wide arc about their points of attachment to the skull, carrying the lower jaw backwards and forwards as they do so.

These subfamilies contain some 75 species all told – 16 in the Pareinae (genera *Pareas* and *Aplopeltura*) and the remainder in the Dipsadinae (genera *Dipsas*, *Sibon* and *Sibynomorphus*). Most of them are nocturnal with large eyes in which the pupil contracts to a vertical ellipse, and many are arboreal, with large heads (much broader than the neck), long slender bodies and proportionally very long tails that may account for as much as a third of the total length – one of the commoner species is known in Trinidad as the 'Fiddle-string snake'. Similar proportions are typical of the majority of climbing colubrids (which never have truly prehensile tails), because greater length, with a long tail to act as a counterpoise, enables them to reach across from branch to branch over wider gaps.

There is a popular belief that almost all snakes will eat eggs, but this is incorrect. A few of them regularly take soft-shelled lizard or snake eggs (Plate 9). The Asiatic *Oligodon* and the Scarlet snake *Cemophora* feed on the contents of lizard, turtle and snake eggs. *Oligodon* can slit the shells with its sharp blade-like maxillary teeth and *Cemophora* seems also to have this ability. However, the brittle shell of a bird's egg is very liable to be broken by a snake's pointed teeth and the contents wasted. Small birds'-eggs are sometimes taken by unspecialized snakes but only the true egg-eating snakes (subfamily DASYPELTINAE) (Plate 8) and some of the rat snakes *(Elaphe)* have special structures for dealing with them. The true egg-eating snakes subsist entirely on hard-shelled eggs; their teeth are reduced both in size and in numbers; there are no more than three or four very small ones on the middle of the lower jaw, four or five at the back of the upper jaw and none at all on the hinder of the two palatal bones (the pterygoid).

The lower jaw is very long, hinging well behind the end of the cranium, and both the supratemporal bones and quadrates are greatly elongated, though they are almost immovably united. This rigidity is further enhanced by the pterygoid bones which are elongated and attached to the lower ends of the quadrates, linking them with the palate and, indirectly, with the upper jaws. In consequence the jaws and palate of each side act in unison, though the two sides can act more or less independently owing to the very great elasticity of the ligament which connects the two halves of the lower jaw at the chin. The palate can be made to slide backwards and forwards by the action of its own intrinsic muscles and these movements are communicated to the lower jaw hinges by the pterygoid bone.

To swallow an egg the snake pushes its open mouth against one end, the egg being prevented from sliding away by a loop of the body, and the jaws, first of one side and then of the other, are pushed forwards and drawn back alternately, the elastic ligament being farther and farther stretched meanwhile, until the whole egg is engulfed. A metre-long snake, with an undistended head scarcely more than 2·5 cm in diameter, can swallow a normal-sized hen's egg. When the egg has been thus swallowed it is broken in the snake's throat by the combined action of the neck muscles and a row of 25–35 special bony projections from the underside of the neck vertebrae.

In the African egg-eaters (*Dasypeltis*), on the first 17–18 vertebrae immediately behind the head, these projections are deep, rectangular blade-like keels that prevent the vertebral column from bending much in the vertical plane, but on the next four to eight vertebrae they are no more than low rounded humps and the neck can be bent up or down in this region. Immediately following this region, the next five to nine vertebrae have long, blunt spurs directed obliquely forwards and downwards and the tips of these prominences, which are capped with very dense, dentine-like bone, project like teeth into the oesophagus and arrest the onward movement of the egg as it is being swallowed. When that has happened the snake bends its head downwards and this movement grips the egg against the 'teeth' which puncture the shell; further muscular contractions result in the complete collapse of the punctured shell, its contents are squeezed onwards into the stomach and after a moment or two the crushed and empty shell is regurgitated.

The six African egg-eaters have no traces of venom grooves on their teeth, but *Elachistodon* of northern Bengal, which is tentatively referred to this subfamily, is 'opisthoglyphous' (Chap. 5) with grooves on the last one or two teeth on each upper jaw. Whether its 'venom fangs' are a completely functionless inheritance is uncertain; its vertebral 'teeth' are less well developed than those of its African counterparts and it may be less exclusively restricted than they are to a diet of eggs.

Another group of specialized colubrids, all of which are technically venomous, with enlarged grooved teeth at the hinder end of the upper jaw, are the aquatic HOMALOPSINAE of the Indo-Australian region. Although these forms have no skeletal modifications to distinguish them from the next subfamily – the typical COLUBRINAE – they differ in many other characters. Their aquatic modifications, though serving similar purposes, differ from those of the equally aquatic wart snakes (Chap. 9). The small eyes are directed more or less upwards and the nostrils, which are crescentic, are situated on the upper surface of the head;

their crescent shape is due to a pad of tissue which encroaches on the hind border of the aperture and which can be distended to close it entirely when diving. To prevent water entering the respiratory passages through the mouth when the nostrils are raised above the surface for breathing, the end of the windpipe (the glottis), which is protrusible, is plugged into the internal opening of the nasal passages.

All the species (34 in ten genera) of the Homalopsinae are essentially aquatic and though most of them frequent fresh waters some are found in river mouths and in coastal waters too. Being to some extent amphibious – coming ashore to bask on beaches and mud-flats – they retain their gastrosteges, but in the Fishing snake, the most completely aquatic member of the group, these structures are obsolescent and it is almost helpless on land. Their venom is not known to be dangerous to human beings though it is presumably toxic to their normal prey which, in most instances, consists of frogs and fish. *Fordonia leucobalia* feeds also on crabs.

The remaining colubrid snakes show varying degrees of adaptation to the vast range of environmental and climatic conditions in which they live. But amongst them there are so many transitional stages between one specialization and another, and there has been so much parallel evolution, with similar modifications arising in different stocks at different times and places in connection with similar needs, that it is difficult to arrange them in further subfamilies. Some groups of genera seem to represent natural assemblages, but their limits are ill-defined and differ according to the criteria employed. For example, some authorities recognize only two major groups – the NATRICINAE and the COLUBRINAE the former being characterized by the possession of spine-like projections (hypapophyses) on the lumbar vertebrae and the latter lacking them; but both conditions occur in some genera (*Boiga, Chrysopelea*).

Form and ornamentation of the hemipenis have also been used as taxonomic characters to define groups, but in some genera such as the Asiatic *Oligodon* and *Plagiopholis* it may be either simple or forked and sometimes the condition is variable even within a single species. So, unsatisfactory though it may be, more than half the world's snakes remain in two subfamilies – the COLUBRINAE and the NATRICINAE.

The more 'typical' colubrines are of medium size, in the 1–2 metre size range, and are active hunters that spend most of their time at ground level. They have a relatively large head, with a distinct neck, and a moderately long tapering tail that usually accounts for between 20 and 30 per cent of the total length. In species that have no clear association with water and do not burrow, the eyes are relatively large and, like the nostrils, are directed laterally, the sides of the head being nearly vertical and the end of the snout square-cut both in plan view and in profile; in diurnal forms the pupil is circular, but in those of nocturnal or crepuscular habits it is often contractile to a vertical ellipse. The more active species tend towards greater length and although many of the racers and whip snakes are of slender build, some of the very large species are almost as robust as boas or pythons; the largest species of all is the Keeled rat snake, of southeastern Asia, which may exceed 3·5 metres, and another exceptionally large form is the Indigo snake (U.S.A. to Brazil), which has been recorded up to 2·9 metres.

Among the colubrines, *Sibynophis* of the Oriental region and *Scaphiodontophis* of South and Central America have a number of unusual features. The hind end of the dentary bone is free from the angular, as it is in the Sunbeam snake, so that a considerable amount of hinging movement is possible between the two bones; and the teeth (which are very numerous – 25 to 56 on each maxilla), instead of being sharply pointed and conical, are compressed and slightly flattened at their tips so that a sharp semicircular or dagger-shaped cutting edge is produced. Such modifications are associated with a diet of hard-scaled lizards such as skinks. These genera become active around dawn, with another but less active period towards dusk, and their movements, unlike those of other snakes, are quick and jerky. Their food is swallowed with incredible speed almost as quickly as it is captured, the very flexible jaws presumably making this possible.

Boomslang and twig snakes

The vast majority of the Colubrinae and Natricinae are harmless to man and two-thirds of them lack any specialized teeth for injecting the secretion of their Duvernoy's glands into their enemies or their prey. The remaining third, however, are opisthoglyphous and while they are seldom injurious to human beings there are two exceptions – the notorious Boomslang (Plate 11) and the twig snake – both of them African tree snakes that subsist mainly on chameleons, other lizards and frogs. These dangerous snakes are unique in having three large functional grooved fangs. These fangs are situated farther forward than in almost any other member of the family and they can inflict an envenomed bite, even on a comparatively large object, with a single stabbing stroke; furthermore their venom is unusually toxic for colubrid snakes (fig. 26).

The forward position of the fangs results from a shortening of the maxillary bone without any compensating decrease in the length of the mouth, a development that has taken place elsewhere for very different reasons, e.g. in the Pareinae and Dipsadinae. In the Boomslang the fangs are preceded by small teeth and, being situated below the centre of the eye, are more nearly comparable in functional position with the fangs of the proteroglyphous and viperid snakes than with those of most colubrines.

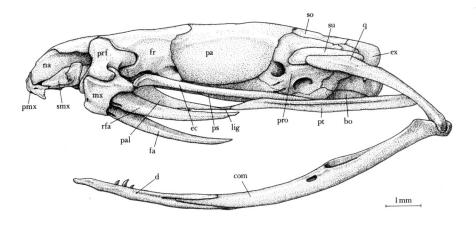

Fig. 27. Skull of aparallactine Mole viper *(Atractaspis aterrima)*. Unlike true vipers, the maxilla and prefrontal in this genus form a complex interlocking joint and the pterygoid lacks teeth. Furthermore there is almost no mobility at the prefrontal/frontal contact, and the pterygoid and palatine bones do not meet. The compactness of the snout bones, loss of postorbital and general streamlining of the skull are probably correlated with the Mole viper's burrowing habits. Key to abbreviations p. 7.

Mole vipers and their allies

The APARALLACTINAE are a clearly defined group of burrowing forms that occur throughout Africa and the Middle East. Small in size, they have a blunt snout, small or minute eyes, no neck constriction, short stumpy tail and a cylindrical body. All of them have a highly developed venom apparatus and the tooth rows on the upper jaws are not only much reduced, with the teeth no farther back than the eye, but in some genera the most posterior ones are deeply grooved. In two genera all the solid maxillary teeth at the front have been lost and only the fangs remain.

Like the elapid snakes there are no pits on the scales, and the loreal scale between the eye and the nostril is absent. They are further distinguished by having a gap between the palatine and pterygoid bones on the roof of the mouth and by the thin soft covering to Duvernoy's gland. The vertebrae behind the heart have no backwardly projecting hypapophyses. The mole vipers, which at one time were thought to be true vipers, are the most remarkable of the aparallactine snakes in their relatively enormous fangs which can be erected independently of each other, and some species have greatly elongated poison glands. The sig-

79

nificance of this development of the venom apparatus is uncertain, but disproportionately large fangs occur in several other genera of burrowing colubrids and very long venom glands are present in the elapine semi-burrowing Malaysian banded coral snake and in at least two species of viper (*Causus*).

Some aglyphous burrowers, like the species of the African genus *Prosymna*, resemble the Aparallactinae in having an equally short maxilla with the hinder teeth greatly enlarged, but there is no corresponding forward movement of these pseudo-fangs which have no venom grooves.

Adaptive radiation in the colubrids

Adaptive radiation from the comparatively unspecialized ground-dwellers takes several paths and some, at least, of these are interconnected. For instance, along one path there is progressively greater association with water – through swamp-dwellers to species that are mainly aquatic – whilst in another direction are the climbing forms with every gradation between those that occasionally clamber amongst the twigs of low bushes, the rock-climbers and those inhabitants of the forest canopy that seldom descend to earth; the two lines are, however, connected by 'arboreal-aquatic' forms that are equally at home in water or in the trees and bushes overhanging it.

Yet another line starting from unspecialized but retiring cryptozoic forms that spend some part of their lives tunnelling through tangles of dense and matted vegetation, culminates in species that lead completely subterranean lives in damp earth; and parallel results have arisen in mud-burrowers of aquatic ancestry. Amongst all such complexities, however, there are some simple, recognizable, adaptive patterns.

Into the water

Aquatic species are usually thick-set, without a distinct neck, and have shorter tails, whilst the eyes are generally smaller and, like the nostrils, are directed obliquely upwards. The nostrils also tend to be closer together, in a more terminal position, and this results in the head plates that separate them (the internasals) being narrower in front and triangular rather than quadrangular in shape or even fused together into a single triangular scute. Being, for the most part, frog- or fish-eaters their teeth are numerous (20–40), and unspecialized, or slightly enlarged posteriorly. All gradations are to be found between dryland and wholly aquatic (freshwater) species and it is probable that the transition from the one environment to the other has taken place on several occasions.

Into the earth

The burrowing line of specialization has some features in common with the aquatic. There is the same reduction in the width of the head, the same thick-set general appearance and even greater reduction of the tail which may be no more than 5–10 per cent of the total length. Eyes, being of little value underground, are always reduced in size and most of the species are themselves small, frequently less than 30 cm in length, though some, which do not construct their own tunnels but live in the burrows of other creatures, may be large and powerful – the African mole snake, for instance, attains a length of more than 2 metres. As in the 'blind' snakes, the snout may be hooked or wedge shaped and the rostral scale is often enlarged and provided with a distinct, angular, 'cutting' edge.

Apart from the burrowing mammals and lizards that are preyed upon by marauding snakes of all kinds, the food available below ground consists mainly of small invertebrates, particularly insects, and it is probably in connection with such hard-shelled prey that many of the small burrowing snakes have acquired disproportionately large, curved, dagger-like 'fangs'.

Into the trees

The keynote of the modifications in climbing and arboreal species is attenuation, because, as noted in connection with the Dipsadinae and Pareinae, they rely on their length to enable them to span the gaps from branch to branch. To prevent overbalancing as they reach out, the fore part of the body is generally very light, the 'neck' being long and slender, and the tail – lengthened to provide a counterpoise – is often between 30 and 45 per cent of the total length. And, to minimise the risk of slipping sideways off the narrow branches along which they have to creep, many species have developed anti-skid arrangements in the form of a pair of angular, raised and keel-like ridges, one on each side of the belly and, sometimes, of the tail, too.

Good vision, with the ability to judge distance accurately, is obviously desirable, if not essential, so that eyes are always well developed and often very large. As mentioned in Chapter 3, some species have acquired binocular vision and the temporal fovea reported in *Ahaetulla* (Plate 9) probably allows it to judge distance accurately.

Into the air

The ability of climbing snakes to ascend vertical surfaces perhaps two-thirds as high as their own length, balancing on the looped last third of the body and making use of every slightest irregularity of the surface, is often quite amazing. Even more unexpected is the ability of some species to jump. This is is accomplished by straightening out with explosive speed from a looped position, and forms like the Golden tree snake of the Orient can spring more than a metre from branch to branch, and even vertically upwards.

The better known accomplishment of this species, however, is indicated by its other name of Flying snake (Plate 11). Launching itself into the air from a high branch, with its body extended and belly drawn in to form a concave surface, it can descend in a steep glide at an angle of 50–60 degrees. To what extent the 'flight' is controlled remains uncertain, but it can abruptly change its direction of descent and one observer has reported that a snake that passed him closely 'came with a furious swimming motion' and landed safely after travelling 50 metres from its starting point in a tree farther up the steep slope on which he was standing.

11 *Cobras and sea snakes*

Cobras, kraits, mambas, coral snakes and sea snakes – Family ELAPIDAE

These snakes seem to represent a single evolutionary stock – the family ELAPI-DAE – which has a more efficient method of injecting venom than any of the Colubridae. As already described (Chap. 5) the fangs are situated at the front of the upper jaw and have an enclosed venom canal instead of an open groove.

With the fangs being anterior to the eyes and in the absence of scale pits and loreal scale the elapids bear characteristics of the aparallactine colubrids, but the two groups differ in a number of features, notably in the venom-producing gland being toughly encapsulated, in the presence, in many of the forms, of teeth behind the fangs, and in the vertebrae having well-developed hypapophyses. In general appearance some elapids bear a strong resemblance to the colubrids.

When or where the elapids originated is not known, but it is clear that they are not a very recent development because fossil cobras are known from deposits of mid-Miocene (14 million years ago). At the present day, they occur widely in the warmer parts of the world and the most primitive types, which have a long upper jaw with a row of smaller teeth behind the fangs, live in the Australian and Papuan regions. In the Australian brown snake, for example, there are between 7 and 15 of these smaller teeth which are grooved like the 'fangs' of the opisthoglyphous colubrids and which may in fact be degenerate fangs, and in the allied genus *Aspidomorphus* there are from 8 to 12 (fig. 28 B). These two genera also have groups of enlarged, fang-like teeth at the front of the lower jaw and these, too, are grooved.

The ancestors of the Elapidae may have had a dentition similar to those rear-fanged colubrids that have an additional tooth behind the grooved fangs (e.g. the African herald snake *(Crotaphopeltis)*), and from them the dentition of the primitive forms may have been derived by a forward shift of the rear fangs, with a consequent loss of the front teeth, and a deepening and enclosing of the grooves of the fangs.

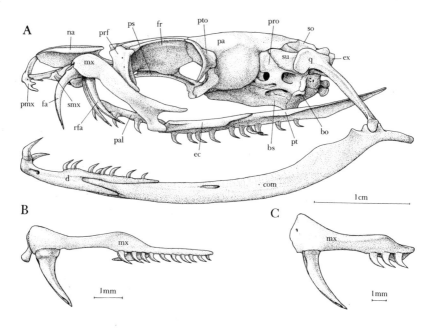

Fig. 28. Variation in maxillary dentition in the Elapidae. A. Skull of the Green forest mamba *(Dendroaspis jamesoni)*. B. Maxilla of *Aspidomorphus lineaticollis*. C. Maxilla of Hamadryad *(Ophiophagus hannah)*. Key to abbreviations p. 7.

Cobras, kraits, mambas and coral snakes

All the members of the Elapidae except the sea snakes are placed in one subfamily, the ELAPINAE. The adaptive radiations of this subfamily are similar to but less extensive than those of the Colubridae – a much larger and, presumably, older group. There are, for example, only two arboreal genera and only one that is thoroughly aquatic. These three are all African, the arboreal forms being the mambas and tree cobras, which are characteristically slender (especially the former), with large eyes and tails that are nearly a quarter of their total length.

The mambas, which have no upper jaw teeth behind the two fangs, have acquired a reputation that is probably exaggerated; they are not aggressive unless provoked or restrained, but they have a very toxic venom, and effective concealing coloration often results in unwitting and too-close surprise encounters. Three of the four species are predominantly green in colour and the fourth, the so-called Black mamba, which is somewhat less arboreal in its habits, is brownish-olive or leaden-grey. The highly toxic tree cobras are confined to the forested regions of equatorial Africa. They are practically hoodless,

84

have huge eyes and are glossy black above and creamy yellow below. Their diet seems to be restricted to frogs.

The water cobras *(Boulengerina)* occur in the fresh waters of the central African region from Cameroun to Lake Nyassa. Despite their almost complete dependence on water – they are almost exclusively fish-eaters – they have no very clear adaptations for life in this element, except that they are heavily built and thick-set, with comparatively small heads on which the eyes and nostrils are somewhat dorsal. Like most of the cobras they have a few small teeth behind the fangs and spread a small 'hood' as a threatening gesture.

The remaining African elapines are either surface-dwellers or semi-burrowers, the latter conforming to the usual pattern of small size (none being more than about 75 cm long), small heads with reduced eyes and short stumpy tails that seldom exceed 10 per cent of the total length; and like many other cryptozoic members of the family in other parts of the world, several of them (Chap. 6) have 'warning' colours, usually consisting of red or yellow cross-bars on a black background.

The much larger and more dangerous surface-dwellers, however, are not brilliantly coloured, though the cobras *(Naja)* and some of their close relatives often disclose a previously concealed pattern of bold black markings when they spread their hoods (Plate 12). There may be broad black cross-bars on the under surface of the neck, as in the Ringhals of southern Africa and most of the six species of cobra that occur in Africa and western Asia, or the more familiar single or double ring-like markings of the eastern 'Cobra-di-capello' whose many races range southwards from the Himalayas and southern China to the Malay Archipelago and Celebes.

The largest venomous snake of all, the Hamadryad *(Ophiophagus hannah)*, which occurs in this same general area of south eastern Asia and is known to reach a length of more than 5 metres, also spreads a small hood; but although it has something of a 'warning' livery in its young stages – black with narrow transverse chevrons or bars of pale yellow on buff – in adults the colouring is dull and procryptic and there are no flash markings.

As its scientific name implies, the Hamadryad (fig. 15) feeds mainly on snakes; and the kraits (Plate 12), which also live in the same area, have a similar diet, but are very different in most other respects. Not only are they much smaller – in the 1–2 metre size range – but they are also mainly nocturnal and have the usual proportions and appearance of secretive snakes; so far from indulging in any aggressive display, when disturbed they coil up into a loose ball (Chap. 6) and only under great provocation can they be induced to bite. Their inoffensive disposition, coupled with the fact that most of the dozen or so species have a striking pattern of black with white or yellow cross-bars, results in there being very few accidents and fatalities are rare.

Some twenty other elapine snakes which resemble the kraits in being nocturnal, inoffensive, cryptozoic and ophiophagous also occur in southeastern Asia. Several of these coral snakes – so called from their warning colours in which red and black are often prominent – indulge in the curious habit of 'head mimicry' (Chap. 6) and one of them, the Oriental coral snake, is remarkable for the enormous development of its venom glands which, instead of being confined to the head region, as in other venomous snakes (except some mole vipers and some night adders), extend so far backwards into the body cavity that they displace the heart. The significance of this is not known.

The only elapines in the New World are also coral snakes which, though of different genera (*Micrurus* (Plate 6) and *Micruroides*), resemble their Old World relatives in many of their ways and in their diet. They have the proportions typical of secretive snakes, and the colouring of all the 30 to 40 species is basically similar, consisting of transverse bars or rings of red, black and yellow or white. In one of the commoner patterns the background colour is sealing-wax red with, at intervals, groups of three black bars separated by two white or yellow rings; but all the species have their own characteristic patterns which differ from one another in the number and relative proportions of the rings and in their arrangement.

Similar, but less highly coloured, 'coral snakes' also occur in the Australian-Papuan region, but in this area, where there are no other competing venomous snakes and few colubrines, the elapines have developed without hindrance and a number of large and potentially more dangerous forms have evolved. The largest of these, the Taipan, may reach a length of over 3 metres, but fortunately it is not a very abundant or widely distributed snake, being found only in the sparsely populated Queensland and New Guinea bush, so that it is not a great menace. Its near relative, however, the Australian copperhead, though appreciably smaller (1 metre), is widespread in the more thickly populated states of Victoria, New South Wales and Tasmania and is consequently more dangerous to man and his domestic animals.

Other dangerous species are the Black snake, the deadly Tiger snake, the Brown snake and the Death adder (Plate 13). The last-mentioned is unusual because, as its name indicates, it looks like a viper (or adder) in a country where there are no vipers. Not only is it viperine in its general appearance, with a broad, flat, triangular head and a stout body, but its habits are not unlike those of the Puff adder, and similar sluggish and cryptically coloured vipers, that rely on escaping the notice of their enemies rather than on flight or on intimidatory display.

Fossil remains of cobras (*Naja*) have been found in France, but no elapines now live in Europe; nor do they exist in Malagasy. Whether they previously inhabited this island is uncertain, but it has been suggested that the evolutionary

86

development and dispersal of the subfamily occurred too late for any to reach Malagasy before it was separated from the main continental land mass. This theory receives support from the absence of the subfamily from other islands, such as those of the Indian Ocean, that were also at one time connected with continents where elapines exist. So, it is all the more remarkable that a single small and perhaps primitive species, *Ogmodon vitianus*, is found in Fiji, and nowhere else, separated by nearly two thousand kilometres of open ocean from its nearest relatives in the Solomon Islands.

Sea snakes

The sea snakes (subfamilies HYDROPHIINAE and LATICAUDINAE), which are amongst the most completely aquatic of all air-breathing vertebrates (Plate 13), differ from the Elapinae only in features that are directly or indirectly concerned with aquatic life. With the exception of a few forms that enter the mouths of rivers and one or two that live in freshwater lakes and lagoons (e.g. *Hydrophis semperi* of Lake Taal in the Philippine Islands and *Laticauda crockeri* of Lake Te-Nggano on Rennel Island) they are all essentially marine. The geographic range of the Yellow-bellied sea snake *(Pelamis platurus)* is wider than that of any other reptile except for some species of sea turtle. Indeed it would be wider still were it not for the cold currents off Namibia and western South America which prevent its passing into the eastern Atlantic and south of the 5° latitude on South America's western seaboard. Unsuitable salinity levels may have excluded it from the Red Sea and this may also be one of the factors that have prevented its reaching the Caribbean through the Panama Canal.

The majority of sea snakes belong to the Hydrophiinae. Their skulls do not differ significantly from those of the elapines, but the dentition is of a relatively primitive type, with short fangs and, except in *Emydocephalus*, a row of smaller solid teeth behind them on the maxilla ; there may be as many as 18 of these *(Hydrophis caerulescens)*. As in most other groups of aquatic snakes (Chap. 4) the eyes are small, and the nostrils which are usually directed almost vertically upwards are provided with a closing mechanism which superficially resembles that of the Homalopsinae. There is a pad of spongy tissue that borders the nostril and can be distended to close it; but whereas the homalopsine pad is hollow, with an opening into its interior, and is situated on the hinder edge of the nostril, that of the sea snake has no opening and borders the nostril anteriorly. To exclude water from the respiratory system when breathing at the surface, the arrangements are, again, similar to those of the homalopsines, the glottis being plugged into the internal opening of the nasal passages.

The most obvious adaptation for life in water, however, is a side-to-side flattening of the hinder part of the body and of the tail which is paddle-shaped with a rounded profile (Plate 13). The gastrosteges are reduced to the vanishing point, or nearly so, in all those that never come ashore and the tongue, whose olfactory function is at a discount under water, is much shorter than in other snakes, only its tips being protrusible through a divided notch in the centre of the upper lip.

Apart from these modifications·associated with an aquatic existence, the overall body form of most sea snakes differs little from typical land snakes. However, some genera (*Microcephalophis*, *Kerilia*) and some species of *Hydrophis* have a tiny head, and a long slender neck that is in marked contrast to the bulk of the posterior trunk. There is also a considerable amount of variation from species to species in the nature of their scales, which may be smooth, or keeled, or warty or even spiny, and in their proportions, from the very slender to the very obese.

While comparatively little is known about the ecology and habits of sea snakes it is clear that these differences in proportions and appearance are associated with different modes of life and specialized feeding habits. Those forms with a normal-sized head and neck feed generally on large eels as well as on a wide range of other fish. The microcephalic species, however, have a strong preference for small eels, especially the Snake and Serpent eels, which they probably capture by thrusting their attenuated heads and necks into crevices in rocks and coral reefs in which these fish lie when not actively feeding. Fish eggs form the staple diet of the wholly marine genera *Aipysurus* and *Emydocephalus*.

Sea snakes are a successful group in the alien environment they have invaded and some of the species occur in vast numbers. From time to time great local concentrations are observed, the surface of the sea being covered with a seething, twisting mass of snakes. On one occasion a belt 3 metres wide and 100 km long was seen from a steamer in the Malacca Strait and the number of individuals of *Astrotia stokesii* in this assemblage must have been astronomical. What causes these events is unknown, though some nuptial connection is suspected.

Yet another unknown biological factor in the lives of marine snakes, and one that does not arise to the same degree in their terrestrial and freshwater relatives, is the method by which they regulate the salt concentration of their blood. In mammals excess salt is removed in solution, mostly in the urine, but in reptiles, as in birds, the amount of liquid excreted by the kidneys is too small to remove any appreciable quantity of salt. Oceanic birds and reptiles that spend part or the whole of their existence in a marine environment take in considerable amounts of salt with their food and they have special 'salt glands' that secrete and discharge a liquid, the salt content of which is well in excess of that of sea water. In sea turtles and in the Galapagos marine iguanas these glands are situated in the eye and nasal regions respectively, but in sea snakes the gland lies in the floor of the mouth surrounding the tongue sheath and its salt secretions are expelled when the tongue is extruded.

The Laticaudinae is currently regarded as being the more primitive group of sea snakes. All have well-developed gastrosteges. The subfamily contains the partly terrestrial *Laticauda*. Two strictly marine genera, *Aipysurus* and *Emydoce-phalus*, have also been referred to this group, but features of the skeleton suggest that they properly belong to the Hydrophiinae. The only oviparous sea snake is *Laticauda*, which returns to land to lay its eggs in crevices on the shore and in caves, at which times it becomes vulnerable to the locals who hunt it for food and for its skin.

The aforementioned Hydrophiinae contains the majority of the 50 or so species of sea snakes. Gastrosteges are vestigial or absent in all except the two more primitive genera (*Ephalophis* and *Hydrelaps*), which may be found foraging on tidal flats or close inshore in very shallow waters.

12 *Vipers*

Fea's viper, true vipers, pit vipers and rattlesnakes – Family VIPERIDAE

The snakes with the most efficient mechanism for injecting venom are the vipers (family VIPERIDAE). As described in Chapter 5, they have long tubular fangs, but no other teeth on the maxillary bone which is shorter than deep and can be rotated through an angle of about 90 degrees on a horizontal axis transverse to the mid line of the head. This rotary movement swings the fangs from a vertical to a horizontal position or vice versa.

It is uncertain when the combination of tubular fangs and a rotating maxilla evolved, but the absence of vipers from the Australasian region suggests that the group may have arisen later in geological time than the Elapidae, which are the dominant snakes of that region. It is, however, almost certain that the family had a northern origin and that subsequently separate lines of evolution arose, in geographical distribution largely complementary with two in the Old World and one in the New.

Fea's viper

The group AZEMIOPINAE contains only Fea's viper *(Azemiops)*, a rare Old World snake restricted to the mountains of southern China, Tibet and Burma and regarded as the most primitive viperid. Superficially it somewhat resembles an elapid or a colubrid snake, its head being covered with a few enlarged and symmetrical plates. *Azemiops* and the Malaysian pit viper are the only members of the Viperidae with all scale rows smooth.

True vipers

The true vipers (subfamily VIPERINAE) differ from the pit vipers in internal anatomy and in lacking temperature-sensitive pit-organs. Further, they are restricted to the Old World where they have undergone a slightly more extensive adaptive radiation than their relatives although none of them inhabits swamps. Currently eight genera are recognized. One genus, *Causus* – the African night adders (Plate 14) – resembles most of the Elapidae and Fea's viper in possessing similar enlarged head plates. A further point of resemblance to the Elapidae lies in the closure of the poison fang canal which is not quite complete; there

90

is a fine line on the surface from base to tip that is a persistent vestige where the lips of the groove from which the canal arose have met and fused.

Another instance of parallel evolution is furnished by the tree vipers of the genus *Atheris* that occur throughout the equatorial forested regions from Liberia to Tanzania and Angola, and which have prehensile tails like the arboreal pit vipers. Some of them have most effective procryptic coloration and behaviour (Chap. 6) and in this respect they contrast markedly with some other vipers of the African forests. The River Jack and the Gaboon viper, for example, though also forest-dwellers but not arboreal, achieve concealment by the diametrically opposite expedient of brilliant and contrasting colours arranged in a disruptive pattern.

The Gaboon viper, and its near relative the Puff adder *(Bitis arietans)* (Plate 15) which occurs in Arabia and in Africa except in the forest regions, are the two largest Old World vipers, reaching a maximum length of nearly 2 metres and a girth comparable with that of a python of similar length. But other species of the same genus living in the arid, near-desert areas of the southwest of the continent are very much smaller; and small size is also characteristic of most of the vipers of the dry zones of northern Africa and southwestern Asia. Amongst the best known of these are the cerastes vipers and carpet vipers (Plate 15), none of which exceeds about 75 cm in length; their adaptations for desert life (e.g. sidewinding locomotion, valvular nostrils and vertical burrowing) and their ability to produce an audible warning by stridulation have already been discussed.

Although mole vipers *(Atractaspis)* possess folding fangs and a venom injecting apparatus they are not true vipers. Their affinities are with the aparallactine group of the Colubridae and are discussed in Chapter 10.

The venomous snakes of Europe are all (with the exception of a single pit viper – *Agkistrodon halys* which reaches the North Caspian region) related to the common Adder (genus *Vipera*) and a few species of this genus also occur in Africa north of the Sahara as well as in Asia. Most of the species are small ground-dwellers that feed principally on rodents, lizards and the like, and their venom is highly toxic for such small creatures. But the human death rate from their bites is comparatively low. Thus, whereas it has been estimated that in Burma, where there are many kinds of venomous snakes, the annual mortality rate may be as high as fifteen per hundred thousand of the population, in Europe as a whole the average number of deaths each year is less than three per ten million; in Britain during the last eighty years only eleven deaths from snake bite have occurred. Nevertheless the bites of even the smaller European vipers are always potentially dangerous and the largest member of the genus, Russell's viper *(V. russelii)*, which ranges from the Himalayas and southern China to Sri Lanka and Indonesia, and reaches a length of more than 1·5 metres, is one of the most deadly snakes of the whole world.

Pit vipers and rattlesnakes

The New World Crotalinae, with six genera (of which two still remain in Asia) are characterized by the possession of a unique type of sense organ which has a thermoreceptor function similar to but more sensitive than the pit on the boid lip. On each side of the head between the nostril and the eye, there is a deep pit, accommodated in a concavity in the side of the maxillary bone and divided into two unequal chambers by a diaphragm (fig. 16). The smaller posterior chamber communicates with the exterior by a narrow duct which, opening near the eye, can be closed by a ring of muscles; this arrangement appears to be a means of controlling and balancing the atmospheric pressure on the two sides of the diaphragm. The much larger anterior chamber has a wide forwardly directed aperture through which infra-red radiations can enter and, if they arise within a certain angular field, fall directly on the diaphragm, which is heat sensitive. Movements of the head will thus enable the snake to ascertain the direction of objects that, being slightly warmer (or colder) than their surroundings, are emitting more (or fewer) heat rays. If the head is oriented so that such an object is directly in front of the snout the radiations will enter both the left and right pit-organs simultaneously to produce a stereo effect that will indicate distance as well as direction. The value of such a system for locating warm-blooded prey and would-be predators, especially at night, is obvious. Experiments have shown that pit vipers, deprived of their senses of sight and smell, can strike accurately at moving objects that are less than 0·2°C warmer than their surroundings. The least specialized of the pit vipers are forms like the Malaysian pit viper and members of the genus *Bothrops* such as the Fer-de-lance and the Jararaca, two greatly feared species which, owing to their wide distribution and relative abundance, are probably responsible for more casualties than any other tropical American snake. A larger and perhaps more dangerous South American pit viper is the Bushmaster *(Lachesis)*, which reaches a length of 3·5 metres and inhabits the humid tropical forest.

Some other American species of *Bothrops* (Plate 16), and several Asiatic representatives of *Trimeresurus* such as the Bamboo and Temple vipers, are more or less arboreal and their adaptation for this environment has followed the same line as in the boas and pythons, and not that of the climbing colubrid and elapid snakes – there is no marked elongation of the body, and the tail instead of being a long counterpoise is relatively short and prehensile.

The greatest modification of the tail, however, occurs in the ground-dwelling rattlesnakes and massasaugas, both of which are essentially North American (though one of the former, the Cascabel *(Crotalus durissus)*, ranges southwards from Mexico to northern Argentina). In these forms a special organ on the tip of the tail produces an audible warning when it is vibrated. It consists of a series of loosely interlocked dumb-bell-shaped, hollow shells each of which was, at

92

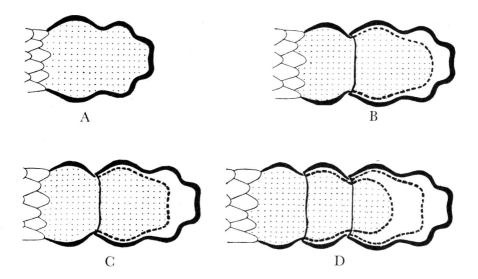

Fig. 29. Development of a rattle (schematic). A. Before the second moult the terminal scale of the tail becomes much thickened. B. After the second moult a new scale grows on the tail-tip inside the old one which was not shed with the rest of the skin. C. Before the next moult the tip of the second 'shell' shrinks. D. After the third moult a third 'shell' grows inside the second.

one stage in its growth, the scale covering the extreme tip of the tail (Plate 16). In other snakes the terminal scale is normally a hollow cone that is barely thicker than the rest of the keratinous layer of the skin and is shed along with it at each successive moult. In rattlesnakes, however, it is a bulb with one or two annular constrictions and is very much thicker than the rest of the horny layer; except at the first moult, immediately after birth, it is not sloughed.

The formation of the rattle is shown schematically in fig. 29. At the second moult the terminal scale becomes loosened, like the rest of the scales, but is not shed because the bulbous new scale growing on the tip of the tail inside it has a greater diameter than the aperture of the old one (fig. 29 B). The tip of the new scale shrinks somewhat before the next moult (fig. 29 C) when, again, a new shell forms on the tail tip inside its predecessor (fig. 29 D); and so on. In this way an extra shell is added to the rattle at each successive moult, but although, in theory, the process should continue indefinitely, in practice the earlier formed shells, towards its tip, wear out and fall off. The rate at which this happens varies with the conditions under which the snake is living and, in nature, the number of shells seldom exceeds fourteen or so, and is often much lower, no matter how old the animal may be; but in the artificial and less turbulent conditions of captivity as many as twenty-nine have been found.

Although the pit vipers are a successful group of animals living under a wide variety of environmental conditions from damp lowland forests to arid deserts and the subarctic zones of very high mountains (Chap. 4) none of them shows any clear specializations for life in water. A few species of the genus *Agkistrodon*, however, and especially the North American Cottonmouth *(A. piscivorus)* are at least partly aquatic, living in or near water and feeding mainly on fish and amphibians. The Cottonmouth is also noteworthy in another connection – it is one of the very few snakes that may be classed as a carrion feeder. In a wild state it has been seen to eat fish heads and entrails thrown away by fishermen.

The eleven families of snakes and some of their characteristics   TABLE 4

	Leptotyphlopidae	Typhlopidae	Anomalepididae	Uropeltidae	Aniliidae	Xenopeltidae	Boidae	Acrochordidae	Colubridae	Elapidae	Viperidae
1 Supratemporal vestigial or absent (compare 7, 15)	+	+	+	+							
2 Quadrate long, inclined forwards (compare 8, 16)	+	+	+								
3 Upper jaw toothless	+										
4 Lower jaw toothless		+									
5 Odontoid absent				+							
6 Hind limbs and pelvis	+			+	+		+				
7 Supratemporal in cranial wall; small				+	+						
8 Quadrate short and vertical				+	+	+					
9 Left lung more than 15% of right				+	+	+	(±)				
10 Coronoid bone	+	+	+	+	+		+				
11 Maxilla mobile on skull		+	+					+	+	+	+
12 Maxilla transversely divided							(+)				
13 Gastrosteges					+	+	+	(−)	+	+	+
14 Brille				(+)	(+)	+	+	+	+	+	+
15 Supratemporal not in cranial wall; often long						+	+	+	+	+	+
16 Quadrate long, inclined backwards						+	+	+	+	+	+
17 Lumbar hypapophyses							(±)	+	(±)	+	+
18 Fixed canaliculate venom fangs										+	
19 Folding canaliculate fangs									(+)		+
20 Tail paddle-shaped										(±)	

On the left are the families of blind, subterranean snakes with small mouths; to the right are the typical and 'advanced' snakes.

Glossary

Adaptive radiation	The development of animals of allied stock along different evolutionary paths in response to differing environments and selective pressures.
Aglyphous	Lacking venom fangs (teeth modified for the injection of venom).
Akinetic	Without mobility; used to describe a skull in which the bones are rigidly connected to one another, precluding movement between them.
Amniote	Any one of those vertebrates (reptiles, birds and mammals) in which the embryo or foetus is enclosed within protective, amniotic, membranes.
Cloaca	The common chamber into which the intestinal, urinary, and reproductive ducts discharge their contents, opening to the outside through the vent.
Crepuscular	Active at dawn or dusk or both.
Cryptozoic	Leading a hidden life, e.g. under stones, bark, leaf litter etc.
Emargination	Notching of the margin.
Epidermis	The outer layers of the skin.
Epithelium	Cell tissue forming the outer layer of mucous membranes and lacking blood vessels.
Gastrosteges	Transversely enlarged scales on the ventral surface of a snake between the head and the scale in front of the vent.
Hemipenis	Either one of the paired male sexual organs of snakes, lizards and amphisbaenians analogous to the penis of mammals.
Integument	The outer covering of the body.
Kinetic	Movable; used to describe a skull in which the bones are loosely attached to one another and capable of considerable independent motion.

96

Loreal scale	Any scale on the side of the head between the scale immediately in front of the eye and the scale or scales bordering the nostril.
Neural spine	The dorsal projection on a vertebra.
New World	The Americas.
Occipital condyle	Bony knob at the back of the skull articulating with the first vertebra.
Old World	The continents of the Eastern hemisphere known before the discovery of the Americas, i.e. Europe, Asia and Africa.
Ophiophagous	Adjective used to describe any animal that feeds on snakes.
Opisthoglyphous	Having venom fangs that are not situated at the front of the mouth.
Oviparous	Egg-laying.
Pentadactyl	Having five digits.
Procryptic coloration	Coloration that camouflages an animal in its natural environment.
Proteroglyphous	Possessing venom fangs on a relatively immovable maxillary bone at the front of the mouth.
Rostral scale	The scale at the tip of the snout forming the anteriormost part of the upper lip.
Scute	Any enlarged scale.
Temporal fovea	An area of acute vision in the upper posterior part of the retina of the eye.
Viviparous	Giving birth to well-developed young. In viviparous reptiles the young break out of the egg as soon as it is laid.

Suggested further reading

BELLAIRS, A. 1969 *The life of the reptiles.* 2 vols. Weidenfeld & Nicolson, London.

BELLAIRS, A. d'A. & ATTRIDGE, J. 1975 *Reptiles.* Hutchinson, London.

BUCHERL, W., BUCKLEY, E. E. & DEULOFEU, V. (editors) 1968 *Venomous animals and their venoms.* Academic Press, New York.

CARAS, R. 1974 *Venomous animals of the world.* Prentice-Hall Inc., Englewood Cliffs, N.J.

DUNSON, W. A. (editor) 1975 *The biology of sea snakes.* University Park Press, Baltimore & London.

GANS, C. 1974 *Biomechanics.* Lippincott, Philadelphia & Toronto.

GANS, C. (BELLAIRS, A. d'A.) & PARSONS, T. S. (editors) 1969 et seq. *Biology of the Reptilia.* Academic Press, London & New York.

GOIN, C. J. & GOIN, O. B. 1971 *Introduction to herpetology.* 2nd. ed. Freeman, San Francisco & London.

HALSTEAD, B. W. (editor) 1970 *Poisonous and venomous marine animals of the world.* Government Printing Office, Washington D.C.

KLAUBER, L. M. 1956 *Rattlesnakes, their habits, life histories and influence on mankind.* 2 vols. University of California Press, Berkeley & Los Angeles.

MERTENS, R. 1960 *The world of amphibians and reptiles.* Harrap, London.

MINTON, S. A. & MINTON, M. R. 1969 *Venomous reptiles.* Scribners, New York.

PARKER, H. W. 1965 *Snakes.* Hale, London.

PORTER, K. R. 1972 *Herpetology.* Saunders, Philadelphia & London.

SCHMIDT, K. P. & INGER, R. F. 1957 *Living reptiles of the world.* Hamish Hamilton, London.

UNDERWOOD, G. 1976 A systematic analysis of boid snakes. In *Morphology and biology of reptiles* (editors A. d'A. Bellairs & C. B. Cox) Linnean Society Symposium Series No. 3.

Index

Figures in **bold** indicate a major reference in the text

99

Top: A primitive worm-like American species, *Leptotyphlops humilis*. The cylindrical body, small head with reduced eyes and short tail are typical of burrowing snakes.
Photo: Nathan W Cohen

Bottom: *Pseudotyphlops philippinus*, a shield-tail of the lowlands of Sri Lanka. The blunt tail, which is larger than the head, has a patch of spines which may help protect the snake against predators.
Photo: Carl Gans

2 Top: The scales of the southeast Asian Sunbeam
snake *Xenopeltis unicolor* have a metallic lustre.
Photo: John H. Tashjian: courtesy Fort Worth Zoo

Bottom: The Rainbow boa *Epicrates cenchria* of the
Neotropics also has highly polished iridescent scales.
Photo: John H Tashjian: courtesy California
Academy of Sciences.

Top: The Emperor boa *Boa constrictor imperator* is a Mexican form of the tropical South American *constrictor*. Unlike pythons well-developed heat detectors on the lips are absent.
Photo: Nathan W Cohen

Bottom: African rock python, *Python sebae*: a juvenile of one of the largest snakes. All boas and pythons are non-venomous and usually kill their prey by constriction.
Photo: J P Coates Palgrave

4 Top: The Malaysian Short python *Python curtus* is readily distinguished from all other pythons by its short body and stocky build.
Photo: John H Tashjian

Bottom: Jayakar's sand boa *Eryx jayakari*, an Arabian species well adapted to living in loose sand. Its colour pattern harmonizes with its surroundings and its eyes being on the top of the head allow the snake to see while lying almost entirely under the sand.
Photo: A G C Grandison

Top: The Calabar ground python *Calabaria
reinhardtii* is a nocturnal, burrowing snake of West
African forests, and is often found in termite nests.
Photo: John H Tashjian: courtesy California
Academy of Sciences.

Bottom: The Asiatic file snake *Chersydrus granulatus* is
found in estuaries and along sea coasts. It is the only
harmless snake that habitually occurs in the sea. Like
its close relative the Elephant-trunk snake it is
persecuted for its granular skin.
Photo: John H Tashjian: courtesy San Diego Zoo
and California Academy of Sciences.

6 The bright colours and patterns of venomous coral
snakes *Micrurus* (above) are apparently imitated by
some harmless species, such as the Milk snake
Lampropeltis doliata nelsoni (below). More striking
similarity is achieved by other species.
Photos: John H Tashjian: courtesy Fort Worth Zoo.

Top: In its defence posture the Rubber boa *Charina bottae* of western North America protects itself by concealing its head among its body coils and 'threatening' its predator with its stumpy tail. Photo: Nathan W Cohen

Bottom: When alarmed the Pacific ring-neck snake *Diadophis punctatus amabilis* coils its tail to expose the brightly coloured undersurface. Photo: Nathan W Cohen

8 Top: The Egg-eating snake of the western forests of Africa *Dasypeltis fasciata*.
Photo: Gerald T Dunger

Bottom: The docile African slug-eater *Duberria lutrix* also feeds on snails.
Photo: Carl Gans

Top: The curious large scale on the snout of the desert patch-nosed snake *Salvadora hexalepis* may be used for rooting out reptile eggs which form part of the snake's diet.
Photo: Nathan W Cohen

Bottom: Oriental whip snake *Ahaetulla nasuta*. This graceful tree snake has a key-hole pupil and long grooved snout which permit a large area of binocular vision.
Photo: Nathan W Cohen

10 Top: A Mexican bull snake *Pituophis deppei*, a typical harmless terrestrial colubrine.
Photo: Charles M Bogert

Bottom: The harmless Eastern hognose snake *Heterodon platirhinos* looks and behaves like a venomous form. It is a past master at playing possum
Photo: John H Tashjian: courtesy California Academy of Sciences.

1 Top: Paradise flying snake *Chrysopelea paradisi*, a
back-fanged snake of southeastern Asia.
Photo: John H Tashjian: courtesy Fort Worth Zoo.

Bottom: Boomslang *Dispholidus typus*, an African
back-fanged arboreal snake in threat attitude. Its
venom is extremely toxic.
Photo: Gerald T Dunger

12 Top: Indian cobra *Naja naja*, in characteristic
threat posture.
Photo: John H Tashjian: courtesy California
Academy of Sciences.

Bottom: Banded krait *Bungarus fasciatus*, a venomous
but generally inoffensive snake of southeastern Asia.
Photo: Govt Press Hong Kong: courtesy John D
Romer

Top: The Death adder *Acanthophis antarcticus* of
Australia resembles and behaves like a viper although
belongs to the cobra group.
Photo: John H Tashjian: courtesy San Diego Zoo.

Bottom: The entirely aquatic Banded sea snake
Hydrophis cyanocinctus. All sea snakes have highly
toxic venom. They occur in the Indian and Pacific
oceans.
Photo: Govt Press Hong Kong: courtesy John D Romer

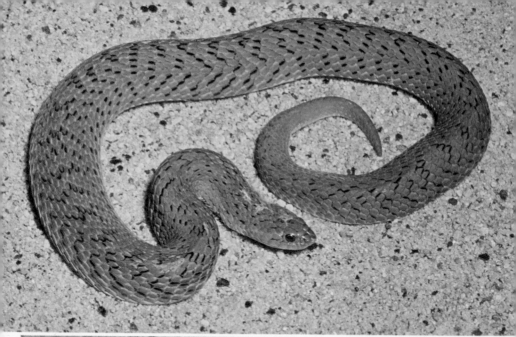

14 Top: Green night adder *Causus resimus*. Unlike
other vipers the African night adders have large
head shields and a round pupil.
Photo: John H Tashjian: courtesy California
Academy of Sciences.

Bottom: Leaf-nosed viper *Eristocophis macmahoni*, an
irascible sidewinder occurring in the West Pakistan
desert areas.
Photo: John H Tashjian: courtesy California
Academy of Sciences.

Top: The African puff adder *Bitis arietans* is a
[dan]gerous, stockily built species. Often found on
[sun-]warmed paths, it is a sluggish creature and does
[not] readily move when approached.
[Pho]to: John H Tashjian: courtesy Fort Worth Zoo.

Bottom: Carpet or Saw-scaled viper *Echis carinatus*.
An extremely dangerous snake in some areas of its
range and responsible for most cases of death from
snake bite in Africa.
Photo: John H Tashjian: San Diego Zoo.

16 Top: The yellow form of the tropical American Eyelash pit viper *Bothrops schlegelii*. An arboreal species that preys on birds and uses its prehensile tail to anchor itself to branches.
Photo: John H. Tashjian: courtesy San Antonio Zoo.

Bottom: The Mexican lance-headed rattlesnake *Crotalus polystictus* is a semi-aquatic medium-sized species found in the mountains of Mexico.
Photo: John H Tashjian: courtesy Houston Zoo.